COMLEX-USA®

LEVEL 1
Lecture Notes 2017
OMM

© 2017 by Kaplan, Inc.

Published by Kaplan Medical, a division of Kaplan, Inc.
750 Third Avenue
New York, NY 10017

10 9 8 7 6 5 4 3 2 1

Course ISBN: 978-1-5062-2158-8

Contributors

Todd Bezilla, D.O.
Wilmington, DE

The editors wish to also acknowledge **Oren Rosenthal, Ph.D., P.T.**, Professor of Anatomy, LECOM College of Osteopathic Medicine.

We want to hear what you think. What do you like or not like about the Notes?
Please email us at **medfeedback@kaplan.com**.

Contents

HISTORY

Osteopathic manipulative medicine (OMM) is a system of medical care with a philosophy that combines the needs of the patient with the current practice of medicine, surgery, and obstetrics, emphasizing the interrelationship between structure and function, and an appreciation of the body's ability to heal itself.

The science of OMM includes the behavioral, chemical, physical, spiritual and biologic knowledge related to the establishment and maintenance of health, as well as the prevention and alleviation of disease. It was founded by Andrew Taylor Still in the late 1800s.

Philosophy

- The body is a unit.
- Structure and function are reciprocally interrelated.
- The body possesses self-regulatory mechanisms.
- The body has the inherent capacity to defend itself and repair itself.
- When normal adaptability is disrupted or when environmental changes overcome the body's capacity for self-maintenance, disease may ensue.
- Movement of fluid in the body is essential for health.
- The nervous system is pivotal to controlling the body.
- There are somatic components to disease that are a result of the disease as well as contribute to the disease process
- Rational treatment is based on these principles.

ORIENTATION TO THE BODY

Planes

- **Sagittal:** divides the body into right and left (side to side)
- **Coronal or frontal:** divides the body into front and back (anterior to posterior)
- **Horizontal transverse:** divides the body into cephalad and caudad (superior to inferior, or top to bottom)

COMLEX Note

Memory Tool

Sagittal = Side to side

Frontal = Front to back

Transverse = Top to bottom

Three Axes of Motion

- Vertical axis or Y axis
- A-P axis or Z axis
- Transverse axis or X axis

Any position can be described in relation to the three cardinal planes and axes.

- **Medial:** toward midline
- **Lateral:** away from midline
- **Prone:** lying facedown
- **Supine:** lying face up

MOTION

Motions are flexion and extension, sidebending, and rotation.

- The point of reference in naming spinal motion is the most anterior superior portion of the vertebral body.
- Coupling refers to motion in which motion or translation of a body about or along one axis is consistently associated with simultaneous rotation or translation about another axis.

Flexion-Extension is motion in a sagittal plane in relation to a transverse axis.

Sidebending (lateral flexion) is motion in the frontal or coronal plane in relation to a horizontal A-P axis. Right sidebending is that condition when the reference point on the anterior superior surface of the vertebral body is moving right. Left sidebending is the converse. Sidebending of the spine results in lateral curves. The terms **convexity** and **concavity** are used to describe the outside and inside of a curve. Sidebending right creates a convexity on the left and a concavity on the right.

Rotation is a general term, but as it relates to spinal motion, the term is reserved for motion in a horizontal or transverse plane in relation to a vertical axis. Right rotation is that condition in which the reference point on the anterior superior surface of the body moves to the right.

Type of movement:

- **Active:** movement produced voluntarily by the patient.
- **Passive:** movement introduced by the operator without patient aid.

Positional description of the spine:

- **Kyphosis:** the A-P curvature of the thoracic spine in the adult, as observed from the side, with the concavity anterior.
- **Lordosis:** the A-P curvature of the cervical and lumbar spine in the adult, as observed from the side, with the convexity anterior.
- **Scoliosis:** a lateral deviation of the spine, as observed from behind.
- **Apex:** the vertebral segment of a group curve that is maximally rotated into the convexity.

Naming Spinal Motion

Spinal motion involves a **vertebral unit**, which is defined as 2 vertebrae with the joint (disc, facets) between.

The direction of spinal motion is named for the superior vertebra relative to the inferior.

Example: T3 in relation to T4

Occiput in relation to atlas

Sacrum in relation to ilium

SOMATIC DYSFUNCTION

Somatic dysfunction is an impairment or altered function of related components of the somatic (body framework) system: skeletal, arthroidial, and myofascial structures and related vascular, lymphatic, and neural elements.

Diagnostic Criteria

Tenderness may be produced during palpation of tissues where it should not occur if there was no somatic dysfunction. A patient with an acute rotator cuff tear will often have exquisite tenderness at the acromion. Pain is sharp and severe. A patient with a chronic rotator cuff tear will often have less pain, characterized as dull and achy.

Asymmetry occurs when bones, muscles, or joints may feel asymmetric to the corresponding structures.

Restriction (*see* Figure 1-1b) means that a joint in somatic dysfunction will have restricted motion—lack of resiliency when you press anteriorly over the transverse process (rotation), laterally (sidebending through translation), or anteriorly at the spinous processes (flexion, extension). To understand restriction, one must understand normal range of motion and barriers associated with normal and abnormal range of motion. *See* "Physiologic and Nonphysiologic Barriers," below.

Tissue texture changes may present in many ways. It is important to understand the differences between acute and chronic somatic dysfunctions.

Acute Somatic Dysfunction Characteristics

- Rubor—red
- Calor—warm
- Dolor—pain
- Tumor—swollen
- Skin drag—moisture (cholinergic activity of sympathetics). In the thoracic spine, these changes are most intense over the costo-transverse articulations.

Chronic Somatic Dysfunction Characteristics

- Fibrosis
- Contracture
- Skin is thin, dry, cool
- Muscles may feel fibrotic

COMLEX Note

Remember diagnostic criteria (TART):

1. Tenderness

2. Asymmetry

3. Restriction

4. Tissue texture changes

Table 1-1. Acute versus Chronic Somatic Dysfunction

Findings	Acute	Chronic
Tenderness	Severe, sharp	Dull, achy, burning
Asymmetry	Present (e.g., paravertebral fullness)	Present with compensation in other areas of the body; obvious rotoscoliosis or increased/decreased spinal curvature (regional lordosis or kyphosis)
Restriction	Present, painful with movement	Present, decreased or no pain
Tissue texture changes	Edematous, erythematous, boggy with increased moisture; muscles hypertonic	Decreased or no edema, no erythema, cool dry skin, with slight tension; decreased muscle tone, flaccid, fibrotic

PHYSIOLOGIC AND NONPHYSIOLOGIC BARRIERS

Under normal physiologic conditions, a joint has 2 barriers:

Physiologic barrier: a point at which a patient can actively move any given joint.

Anatomic barrier: a point at which a physician can passively move any given joint. Note: Any movement beyond the anatomic barrier will cause ligament, tendon, or skeletal injury.

In somatic dysfunction, a joint will have a **restrictive** (or **pathologic**) **barrier** (*see* Figure 1-1b). A restrictive barrier lies before the physiologic barrier and prevents full active and passive range of motion of that joint. For example, a patient may have a full range of motion for rotation of the neck to the right. However, the patient may only be able to turn his head to the left approximately 70°. Therefore, a restrictive barrier is met when turning the head to the left.

COMLEX Note

Know the difference between **physiologic**, **anatomic**, and **restrictive barriers**.

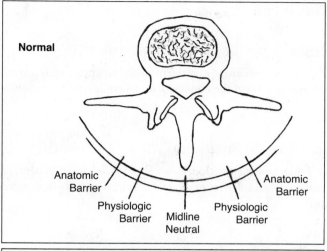

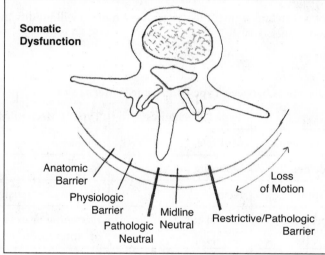

Figure 1-1a (*top*). In a vertebral segment without somatic dysfunction, the vertebrae may rotate equally to either side. **Figure 1-1b** (*bottom*). If somatic dysfunction is present, the vertebral segment will not lie in the midline position, and the patient will not be able to rotate the vertebral segment past the restrictive (or pathologic) barrier.

COMLEX Note

Fryette's principles I and II apply only to the **thoracic** and **lumbar vertebrae**, not to the cervical vertebrae.

FRYETTE'S PRINCIPLES

Principle I (Neutral Position; Type I Mechanics)

When the spine is in a neutral position (easy normal) and sidebending is introduced, the **bodies of the vertebrae** will rotate toward the convexity (sidebending and rotation occur in opposite directions).

Principle II (Non-Neutral Position; Type II Mechanics)

When the spine is in a **non-neutral position**, either forward or backward bent, and sidebending is introduced, **a singular vertebra** will rotate toward the concavity (sidebending and rotation occur in the same direction).

Principle III (Type III Mechanics)

Initiation motion of a vertebral segment in any plane of motion will modify the movement of that segment in other planes.

Table 1-2. Differences between Type I and Type II Mechanics

	Type I Mechanics	Type II Mechanics
Number of segments	Multiple	Single
Rotation/side bending	Opposite side	Same side
Position of spine	Neutral	Flexion or extension
Clinical appearance	Lateral curve	Flattening or exaggeration of anteroposterior curve
Onset	Usually gradual	Usually abrupt

SYMPATHETIC NERVOUS SYSTEM

Table 1-3.

Visceral Organ	Sympathetic Innervation	Parasympathetic Innervation
Head and neck	T1–T4	Cranial nerves III, VII, IX, X
Heart	T1–T5	Vagus n.
Respiratory system	T2–T7	Vagus n.
Esophagus	T2–T8	Vagus n.

Upper GI tract
   Stomach
   Liver
   Gallbladder
   Spleen
   Portions of the pancreas and duodenum
	T5–T9	Vagus n.

Middle GI tract
   Portions of the pancreas and duodenum
   Jejunum
   Ileum
   Ascending colon
   Proximal 2/3 of transverse colon
	T9–T12	Vagus n.

Lower GI tract
   Distal 1/3 of transverse colon
   Descending colon
   Sigmoid colon
   Rectum
	T12–L2	S2–S4

Kidneys	T11–L1	Vagus n.
Upper ureters	T10–L1	Vagus n.
Lower ureters	L1–L2	S2–S4
Urinary bladder and urethra	T11–L2	S2–S4
Gonads	T10–T11	Vagus n.
Uterus and cervix	T10–L2	S2–S4
Erectile tissue of penis or clitoris	T11–L2	S2–S4
Extremities Arms	T5–T7	None
Legs	T10–T12	None

COMLEX Note

Segmental sympathetic innervation varies from individual to individual and consequently will vary from author to author. There is no need to memorize the exact innervation for all the organs; rather, become familiar with the region of the spinal cord that innervated the viscera.

Here's an easy way to understand the sympathetic innervation to organ systems:

> Head and neck = T1–T4
>
> Heart = T1–T5
>
> Lungs = T2–T7
>
> GI tract = T5–L2
>
> > Remember two landmarks:
> >
> > - Ligament of treitz
> > - Splenic flexure
>
> Anything in between the ligament of treitz and the splenic flexure is innervated by T9–T12. Anything proximal is T5–T9. Anything distal is T12–L2.
>
> More important points:
>
> - The spinal cord ends at L2, as does the sympathetic chain ganglia. Therefore, nothing comes from L3–L5.
> - Autonomic innervation varies slightly depending on the author. The largest discrepancy involves the autonomic innervation to the arms. The Foundations text lists T5–T7, whereas Kuchera's *Osteopathic Principles in Practice* lists T2–T8.

NAMING AND EVALUATING SOMATIC DYSFUNCTIONS

Naming Somatic Dysfunctions

When referring to segmental motion or restriction, refer to the upper of the two vertebrae in a functional vertebral unit or segment.

Relative freedom of motion

The osteopathic physician determines the freedom of motion based on the ease of motion and restriction of motion in the different planes (flexion, extension, rotation, and lateral sidebending) by the vertebral unit or its segments. Positional change is named for the direction of free motion.

Three examples:

- If L2 is restricted in the motions of flexion, sidebending to the right and rotation to the right, then L2 is said to be extended, rotated, and sidebent to the left on L3. This is denoted as L2 ER_LS_L or ERS_L.

- If T5 is restricted in the motions of extension, sidebending to the left and rotating to the left, then T5 is said to be flexed, rotated, and sidebent to the right on T6. This is denoted as T5 FR_RS_R or FRS_R.

- If T1 is not restricted in flexion or extension but is restricted in sidebending to the left and rotating to the right, then T1 is said to be neutral, sidebent right, and rotated left. This is denoted as NSR_L or NS_RR_L.

Evaluating Spinal Somatic Dysfunctions

Cervical spine

See following chapter.

Thoracic and lumbar spine

1. **Assess rotation by placing the thumbs over the transverse processes of each segment**. If the right thumb is more posterior than the left, then the segment is rotated right.
2. **Check the rotation of the segment in flexion**. If the rotation gets better (i.e., the right thumb is no longer posterior), this suggests that the segment is flexed, sidebent, and rotated right (FR_RS_R).
3. **Check the segment in extension**. If the rotation gets better in extension, this suggests that the segment is extended, sidebent, and rotated right (ER_RS_R). If the rotation remains the same in flexion and extension, then the segment is neutral, sidebent left, and rotated right (NS_LR_R).

The human spine can move in three planes or any combination thereof. Each plane corresponds with a particular axis and motion.

Table 1-4

Motion	Axis	Plane
Flexion/Extension	Transverse	Sagittal
Rotation	Vertical	Transverse
Sidebending	Anterior–posterior	Coronal

Osteopathic Treatment

Direct versus indirect treatment

In a **direct treatment**, the practitioner "engages" the restrictive barrier. This means that the body tissues and/or joints are moved closer to the restrictive barrier.

In an **indirect treatment**, the practitioner moves tissues and/or joints away from the restrictive barrier.

Passive versus active treatment

In an **active treatment**, the patient will assist in the treatment, usually in the form of isometric or isotonic contraction.

In a **passive treatment**, the patient will relax and allow the practitioner to move the body tissues.

In a **neuroreflexive treatment**, various reflexes, such as Chapman's reflexes, abdominal ganglia, etc., are stimulated to induce changes.

In a **mechanical action treatment** (articulatory techniques), specific repetitive motions are performed to produce specific and general effects, i.e., lymphatic pumps.

Table 1-5

Treatment Type	Direct or Indirect	Active or Passive
Myofascial release	Both	Both
Counterstrain	Indirect	Passive
Facilitated positional release	Indirect	Passive
Muscle energy	Direct (rarely indirect)	Active
High-Velocity Low Amplitude (HVLA)	Direct	Passive
Lymphatic treatment	Direct	Passive
Cranial osteopathy	Both	Passive

Treatment plan

Precise answers to choice of technique do not exist; there are only general guidelines:

- Elderly patients and hospitalized patients typically respond better with indirect techniques or gentle direct techniques, such as articulatory techniques.
- Acute neck strain/sprain is often better treated with indirect techniques to prevent further strain.
- Patients with advanced stages of cancer should not be treated with lymphatic techniques due to the increased risk of lymphogenous spread.
- Patients with osteoporosis, rheumatoid arthritis, and bone cancer should not be treated with HVLA.

Dose and frequency:

- The sicker the patient, the lower the dose.
- Pediatric patients can be treated more frequently as compared with geriatric patients.
- Acute dysfunction can be treated with more frequent sessions.

Sequencing of treatment:

- Treat the thoracic spine before treating rib dysfunctions.
- For extremity problems, treat the axial skeleton first, then work proximal to distal to assist in the drainage of the edema.
- Attempt to find and treat primary problems first, then secondary problems later.

COMLEX Note

Myofascial release is the only treatment that is either direct or indirect and either active or passive.

COMLEX Note

Memory Tool
Treat the worst first.

BONES

The **occiput** serves as the connection between the skull and the cervical spine. The occipit has two convex condyles that fit into the concave superior articular facets of the atlas. **The major motions of the occipito-atlantal (OA) joint are flexion and extension**. OA joint motion accounts for 50% of the flexion and extension of the cervical spine. The minor motions are side-bending and rotation. The occipital condyles converge anteriorly. This relationship is important when considering treatment of occipital dysfunction. The occiput sidebends and rotates to opposite sides. When the occiput sidebends to the right it rotates to the left (and vice versa; Fryette's principle I mechanics).

The **atlas (C1)** does not have a vertebral body. This bone has two kidney bean–shaped superior articular facets that articulate with the occipital condyles. The atlas articulates with the axis (C2) via the odontoid process. It also has two inferior facets that articulate with the superior facets of the axis. **The major motion of the atlas-axis (AA) joint is rotation**. Around 50% of the normal rotation of the cervical spine occurs at the AA joint.

C2–C7 are known as the typical vertebrae. Each has a body, 2 superior facets, and 2 inferior facets. The facet joints of C2–C7 are angled superiorly and anteriorly at a 45° angle. This relationship is important to remember when applying corrective techniques. Typical cervical vertebrae (C2–C7) normally sidebend and rotate to the same side. These vertebrae account for the remaining 50% of the flexion/extension and sidebending/rotation of the cervical spine.

ABOUT THE CERVICAL SPINE

The articular pillars (or lateral masses) are the portion of bone of the cervical vertebral segments that lie between the superior and inferior facets. The articular pillars are located posterior to the cervical transverse processes and are used by osteopathic physicians to evaluate cervical vertebral motion. Foramen transversarium are foramina in the transverse process of C1–C6 that allow for the passage of the vertebral artery. The vertebral artery does not pass through the foramen transversarium of the C7 vertebra.

Clinical Correlate

Headaches are often found to be caused, in part, by cervical dysfunctions, i.e., greater occipital nerve irritation.

COMLEX Note

- The angle created by the articular pillars (facet joints) determines, in part, the motion characteristics of the cervical spine.

- Abnormal anatomy, whether it is congenital or acquired, may cause somatic dysfunction.

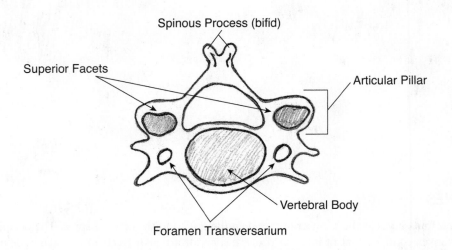

Figure 2-1. Typical Cervical Vertebra

Muscles

Suboccipital muscles—include the rectus capitis posterior major, rectus capitis posterior minor, obliquus capitis inferior and the obliquus capitis superior. The jugular vein is responsible for 90% of the venous drainage from inside the head. The internal jugular vein exits the head from the jugular foramen and runs through the suboccipital region. Excessive contraction (tension) in the suboccipital muscles may interfere with venous drainage from the head and may produce symptoms of congestion (sinusitis). The suboccipital muscles are frequently found to be tight in patients suffering from tension headache. Proper treatment of this region may decrease the discomfort associated with tension headache.

Scalenes—the anterior, middle, and posterior scalenes are important to proper functioning of the cervical spine. The brachial plexus and subclavian artery lie between the anterior and middle scalene muscles. Dysfunction of these two muscles may produce symptoms in the upper extremity.

Sternocleidomastoid—covers the great vessels of the neck and the cervical plexus of nerves. Dysfunction in this muscle may produce dysfunction in underlying structures. This muscle originates on the manubrium of the sternum and the medial third of the clavicle. It inserts into the mastoid process of the temporal bone. Unilateral contraction sidebends the head to the same side and rotates it to the opposite side. Example: contraction of the right sternocleidomastoid muscle will sidebend the head to the right and will rotate the head to the left so that the face is turned superiorly. Bilateral contraction produces flexion of the neck.

Vasculature

Carotid arteries—the carotid arteries run through the cervical region and enter the skull via the carotid canal. The internal carotid arteries supply the anterior portions of the cerebrum. Dysfunction affecting these arteries may produce symptoms on the opposite side of the body (weakness, altered sensation, etc.). The carotid sinus is a slight dilation of the proximal part of the internal carotid artery. The carotid sinus responds to an increase in arterial pressure by slowing the heart rate (via parasympathetic outflow associated with the vagus nerve). Pressure on the carotid sinus may produce syncope. Cervical restrictions may interfere with blood flow to structures distal to the restriction.

Clinical Correlate

Double Crush Syndrome occurs when there is a proximal compression on a nerve (scalenes on the brachial plexus), allowing a distal nerve compression to manifest symptoms more readily (median nerve entrapment at the wrist flexor retinaculum [carpal tunnel syndrome]).

Torticollis occurs when the sternocleidomastoid (unilaterally) is in spasm. It may be caused by trauma to the accessory nerve (CN XI) or cervical plexus. It causes the head to sidebend and rotate in opposite directions, i.e., a right torticollis causes the head to sidebend right and rotate left.

Vertebral arteries—arise from the subclavian artery, ascend through the transverse foramen of cervical vertebrae, and enter the skull through the foramen magnum. The vertebral arteries unite to become the basilar artery at the level of the pons. The basilar artery crosses the pons and ends by giving off 2 posterior cerebral arteries at the level of the cerebrum. The vertebral arteries supply blood to the visual area of the cerebrum (occipital lobe), the brain stem, and the cerebellum. Dysfunctions affect this artery may result in visual abnormalities, dizziness, and other problems.

COMLEX Note

Care must be used to not compromise the vertebral artery during cervical evaluation and manipulation. Try to avoid positions combining extension with side bending and rotation.

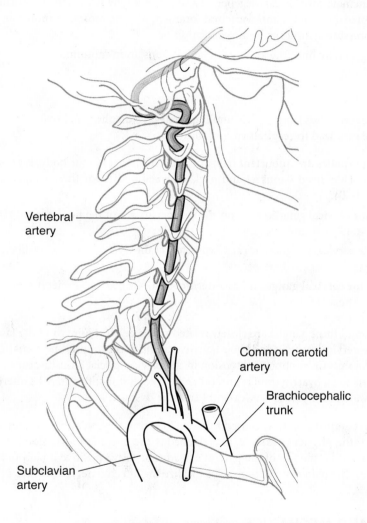

Figure 2-2. Vertebral Arteries

Ligaments

The **alar** ligament extends from the sides of the dens to the lateral margins of the foramen magnum and limits rotation. The **transverse** ligament of the atlas attaches to the lateral masses of C1 to hold the dens in place.

Joints

Joints of Luschka (uncovertebral joints) are formed by the uncinate process of the inferior vertebrae and the vertebral body of the superior vertebrae. They are not considered synovial joints. They are involved in cervical motion, especially sidebending, and are important for the following reasons:

- They act as barriers to prevent extrusion of disc material posterior laterally onto nerve roots.
- The uncinate process can degenerate and hypertrophy with arthritis. Because of the close proximity of the intervertebral foramen, it is the most common cause of nerve root pressure symptoms in the cervical spine.
- They generally limit the amount of lateral translation motion.

Nerves

The **phrenic nerve** arises from C3–C5 and innervates the diaphragm. Dysfunction affecting the phrenic nerve may lead to respiratory complications.

Cervical sympathetics are important in sympathetic responses in the body, especially the heart and structure of the head (sinuses) and neck. The cell bodies for these ganglia are located at spinal levels T1–T4.

- **Inferior cervical ganglion** lies on the ventral surface of the head of the first rib. It sends fibers to C7, C8, and T1.
- **Middle cervical ganglion** lies approximately at the level of C6. It sends fibers to C5 and C6.
- **Superior cervical ganglion** lies anterior to the C1–C2 vertebrae. It sends fibers to cervical nerves C1–C4.

The fascia around these ganglia are closely related to the cervical joints and the fascial planes of the neck. The cervical ganglia and their activity can be compromised by somatic dysfunction in the cervical joints or by abnormal tension in the cervical fascia. Sinusitis, ear or eye dysfunctions, and cardiac tachyarrhythmias and other cardiac dysfunctions may be altered by freeing cervical pathways and treating cervical joint somatic dysfunctions.

Spurling test (compression test) is used to assess for cervical nerve root compression. With the patient seated, the physician extends and sidebends the C-spine to the side being tested and pushes downward on the top of the patient's head. The test is positive if pain radiates into the ipsilateral arm. The pain distribution helps localize the affected nerve root.

MOTION AND MECHANICS

Neck pain, headache, vertigo, and upper extremity symptoms referred from the cervical region are common patient complaints and are sources of functional disability.

Occipito-Atlantal (OA) Joint (Sidebending Focus)

The occiput rotates opposite to the direction of sidebending. When the occiput sidebends to the right, it rotates to the left (and vice versa). Translation of the occiput to the left produces sidebending to the right and rotation to the left.

Clinical Correlate

Diaphragm irritation can cause cervical dysfunction via the phrenic nerve.

Mnemonic

C3, C4, C5 keeps the diaphragm alive

Occipital motions are small; therefore, apply small, carefully directed forces. For example, the occiput translates freely to the left (sidebends right) and has a restriction to the right translation (sidebending left). The occiput is therefore sidebent right and rotated left.

Atlanto-Axial (AA) Joint (Rotational Motion)

The major motion of the atlas is rotation. Dysfunctions are named for the direction of freer motion. To assess the motion of the atlas, hold both sides of the patient's head with your hands. Attempt to place the tips of your index and middle fingers over the lateral aspects of the atlas. Then, flex the patient's cervical spine by lifting the head off the table. This will lock C2–C7 and help localize motion to the atlas. While maintaining this position, turn the patient's head to the right and to the left. Use the patient's chin as a landmark and determine which direction moves more freely and which direction has restricted motion. Also, feel the motion of the atlas with your fingertips. If the head moves more freely to the left, the AA is said to be rotated left (and vice versa).

C2–C7 (Fryette's Principle II Mechanics)

Sidebending and rotation should occur to the same side. Cervical vertebrae can be flexed, extended, or neutral. The primary motion for the upper cervicals (C2–C4) is rotation. The primary motion for the lower cervicals (C5–C7) is sidebending.

Two tests are used to assess vertebral motion in this region:

Rotational test: Position your fingers posterior to the transverse processes/lateral masses of a typical cervical vertebra. Introduce rotation to the left and the right along a plane directed up toward the eye. Palpate the quality of motion with your finger. Determine the direction of freer motion.

Translational test: This is used to assess sidebending. Position your fingers lateral to the transverse processes of the typical cervical vertebra being tested. Translate the vertebra to the right and to the left while palpating the quality of motion. Remember, translating the vertebra to the right introduces sidebending to the left, and vice versa. Determine the direction of freer motion.

IMPORTANT CONSIDERATIONS ABOUT THE CERVICAL SPINE

Suboccipital or paravertebral muscle spasms are often associated with upper thoracic or rib problems on the same side. Therefore, treat these areas first if dysfunction is present; then treat the cervical spine. Treating the upper thoracic segments as well as the ribs may alter sympathetic influence to the head and neck structures. Normalizing sympathetic tone will help reduce muscle tone and allow these areas to relax.

An acute injury to the cervical spine (whiplash) is best treated with indirect fascial techniques or counterstrain first. In an acute injury, cervical muscles still may be in spasm; direct techniques such as HVLA is contraindicated because sudden movements may cause further muscle strain.

Forward bending of the c-spine causes the nucleus pulposus to be pushed further posteriorly. If forward flexion exacerbates a person's symptoms (especially if the symptoms included paresthesias and weakness in a particular dermatome and myotome), it is indicative of a herniated nucleus pulposus. Electromyography or MRI may confirm the findings.

Backward bending of the c-spine will close the intervertebral foramen. If backward bending further produces a patient's symptoms (neurologic symptoms in the shoulder or arm), it is indicative of cervical foraminal stenosis. Use the Spurling test. Note: Symptoms must radiate below the shoulder for the Spurling test to be positive. Oblique x-rays of the cervical spine are used to visualize vertebral foramina and will therefore help diagnose foraminal stenosis.

Latissimus dorsi

The latissimus dorsi originates from the spinous processes of T6–T12, iliac crest, and Ribs 8 (9)–12. Inserts through the humerus. It extends, adducts, and medially rotates the humerus. It is also thought to elevate Ribs (8) 9–12 with deep inspiration.

Nerves

- Brachial plexus
- Autonomics (sympathetics)
  - T1–T4: head, neck
  - T1–T6: heart, lungs
  - T5–T9: stomach, duodenum, liver, gall bladder, pancreas, and spleen
  - T10–T11: small intestine, kidneys, ureters, gonads, R colon
- Intercostals

Blood Vessels and Lymphatic Flow

- Internal thoracic (mammary) artery and vein; intercostal artery and vein
- Lymphatics from lower body, trunks from left head, arm, and thoracic viscera—all drain through thoracic duct to the left subclavian (internal jugular junction). The rest drains to the right internal jugular (subclavian junction).

RIBS

Typical Ribs Versus Atypical Ribs

What makes a typical rib typical? If a rib has the following 5 components, it is labeled as typical.

- Tubercle
- Head
- Neck
- Angle
- Shaft

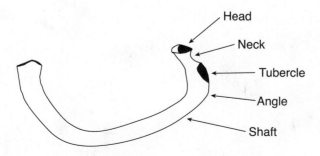

Figure 3-1. Typical Rib

Mnemonic

All atypical ribs have the number 1 or 2.

Typical ribs: 3–10

Atypical ribs: 1, 2, 11, and 12. These ribs are labeled atypical because they either lack the above-mentioned components or have other distinguishing characteristics.

Note: Sometimes Rib 10 is considered atypical.

True, False, and Floating Ribs

COMLEX Note

Know the difference between true, floating, and false ribs.

- True = Ribs 1–7; connect to the sternum by their costal cartilages
- False = Ribs 8–10; do not directly connect to the sternum (or do not attach at all)
- Floating = Ribs 11–12

Rib Motion

There are 3 classifications of rib movement:

- **Pump-handle motion** (*see* Figure 3-2a) increases the anterior-posterior dimension of the thorax. The anterior ends of the ribs rise, causing the sternum to rise.
- **Bucket-handle motion** (*see* Figure 3-2c) increases the transverse diameter of the thorax. With inhalation, these ribs ascend and move laterally.
- **Caliper motion** (*see* Figure 3-2b): with inhalation these ribs move posterior and laterally

Note: All ribs have a varying proportion of these motions depending on their location within the ribcage.

- The upper ribs (**Ribs 1–5**) move *primarily* in a pump-handle motion.
- The middle ribs (**Ribs 6–10**) move *primarily* in a bucket-handle motion.
- The lower ribs (**Ribs 11 and 12**) move *primarily* in a caliper motion.

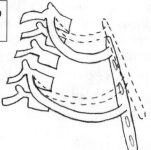

Dotted lines show rib position in inhalation

Figure 3-2a. Pump-Handle Movement of Ribs 1–5

Dotted lines represent rib position in exhalation

Figure 3-2b. Caliper Motion of Floating Ribs

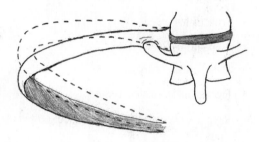

Figure 3-2c. Bucket-Handle Movement. A posterior–anterior view of a midthoracic rib. Note that with inspiration, the rib moves up, similar to a bucket-handle.

Rib Dysfunction

Inhalation dysfunction

Older terminology is "exhalation restriction." Because ribs move cephalad with inhalation, a rib inhalation dysfunction occurs when one rib or a group of ribs get "stuck" in the inhalation position (ribs "stuck up"). Pump-handle ribs will be positioned up anteriorly and bucket-handle ribs will be positioned up laterally.

Exhalation dysfunction

Older terminology is "inhalation restriction." Because ribs move caudad with exhalation, a rib exhalation dysfunction occurs when one rib or a group of ribs get "stuck" in the exhalation position (ribs "stuck down"). Pump-handle ribs will be positioned down anteriorly and bucket-handle ribs will be positioned down laterally.

COMLEX Note

Know the 3 classifications of rib movement and the ribs involved in each type of motion.

COMLEX Note

Know the difference between inhalation and exhalation rib dysfunctions.

Clinical Correlate

- A patient complaining of chest pain upon breathing indicates a rib dysfunction.

- Pain on inhalation = exhalation dysfunction

- Pain on exhalation = inhalation dysfunction

COMLEX Note

Know the "key" rib in group somatic dysfunctions.

Group Dysfunction

Group dysfunction occurs when two or more ribs are positioned in the inhalation (group inhalation dysfunction) or exhalation (group exhalation dysfunction). In these cases, there is usually one rib that is responsible for causing the dysfunction. This rib is referred to as the "key" rib. It is important to direct treatment toward the key rib.

- In inhalation dysfunctions, the key rib is the lowest rib of the dysfunction.
- In exhalation dysfunctions, the key rib is the uppermost rib of the dysfunction.

Clinical Correlate

Idiopathic Scoliosis:

- Most common type of spinal deformity
- Hypokyphotic disease

Screening Tool:

- Adam's forward bending test
- Scoliometer

Curve Patterns:

- Right thoracic (most common)
- Right shoulder rotated forward
- Right scapula medial border protrudes posteriorly

Treatment—3 "O"s

- Cobb angle $< 30°$ → observation
- $30°$ to $40°$ → orthosis (bracing) during growing years
- $> 40°$ → operative (surgery)

ANATOMY

There are 5 lumbar vertebrae distinguishable by their large quadrangular spinous processes. The large cross-sectional area of the lumbar vertebral body is designed to sustain longitudinal loads.

In the thoracic and lumbar region a nerve root will exit the intervertebral foramen below its corresponding segment. The lumbar nerve roots exit the superior aspect of their corresponding intervertebral foramina, just *above* the intervertebral disc. This information is important when considering disc herniations (discussed later).

The spinal cord ends at approximately the level of L2.

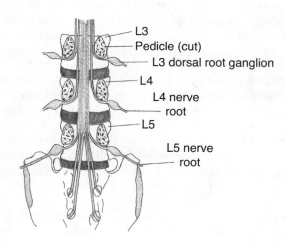

Figure 4-1. Lumbar nerve roots exit intervertebral foramen below the corresponding segment but above the intervertebral disc.

Anatomic Variations

Sacralization

Sacralization is bony conformation in which one or both of the transverse processes of L5 fuse with the sacrum. The disk space between the sacralized vertebra and sacrum is usually narrow. Sacralization occurs in about 3.5% of the population. It is more often bilateral than unilateral. This may increase stability of the lumbosacral junction, placing enormous strain on the joints above, leading to disk degeneration.

Lumbarization

Lumbarization is the failure of S1 to fuse to the remaining portion of the sacrum during development. It will result in what appears to be a sixth lumbar vertebrae.

Spina bifida

Spina bifida is a developmental abnormality of the neural tube in which the 2 halves of the vertebral arch fail to fuse. The severity of the condition varies depending on the degree of malformation.

- **Spina bifida occulta** is a failure of fusion of the posterior bony elements of the spine with intact thecal sac and normal spinal cord, and usually a patch of hair over the site involved. There is no associated neurologic deficit. Normal variant seen on 5–10% of the population.
- **Spina bifida meningocele** (cystica) is a failure of fusion of the posterior bony elements. Cystic outpouching of the thecal sac filled with CSF, but no spinal cord or nerve disruption, with or without intact skin, so no neurologic deficits.
- **Spina bifida meningomyelocele** is a significant disruption of all elements of bony spine with open, malformed neural tube with membranous sac. Associated with variable degree of neurologic defects.

Muscles

Erector spinae group is the spinalis, longissimus, and iliocostalis. Large muscle forms a prominent bulge on each side of the vertebral column. It lies within a fascial compartment between the posterior and anterior layers of the thoracolumbar fascia. It is arranged in three columns: the iliocostalis (lateral column), longissimus (middle column), and spinalis (medial column).

Multifidus and **rotators** are the deep muscles of the back. Multifidi span 2–4 vertebrae. The rotators arise from the transverse process of one vertebra and insert onto the base of the spinous process of the vertebra superior to it. Rotators span either 1 or 2 vertebrae.

Quadratus lumborum originates from the medial half of the 12th rib and tips of the lumbar transverse processes and inserts onto the iliolumbar ligaments and the internal lip of the iliac crest. It extends and sidebends the lumbar spine (ipsilaterally). It also fixes the 12th rib during inspiration.

Iliopsoas consists of the psoas portion, which originates from the transverse processes and vertebral bodies of T12–L5, and the iliacus portion, which originates from the iliac fossa. The iliopsoas inserts on the lesser trochanter of the femur. It is the primary flexor of the hip and also serves as an external rotator of the lower extremity.

Lumbar Mechanics and Somatic Dysfunction

Due to the alignment of the facets (backward and medial for the superior facets), **the major motion of the lumbar spine is flexion and extension**. There is a small degree of sidebending and a very limited amount of rotation. Motion of the lumbar spine will follow Fryette's principles. Somatic dysfunction may occur in any of the three planes of motion.

COMMON PROBLEMS CAUSING LOW BACK PAIN

Somatic Dysfunctions of the Lumbosacral Spine (Back Strain)

A back strain is an acute soft tissue injury accompanied by pain in the lumbar region. Symptoms may begin, followed by an episode of mild trauma, especially twisting. The strain may become chronic. Patients report a mild history of muscle ache or spasm in their lower back. On examination, the patient will have discrete tender points in the lumbar region and surrounding tissues. There may be a compensatory curve elsewhere in the spine. Often, somatic dysfunction is present. There are no neurologic defects.

Osteopathic manipulative therapy (OMT) can be of great value in this type of condition. Treatment may vary with the level of acuteness. Initial treatment should be gentle and indirect, followed by more direct techniques. Treating L5 before the sacrum is a general guideline. In acute situations, treat surrounding tissues to allow you to gain access to the acute area. Evaluate patients for lumbar tender points.

Clinical Correlate

The most frequent direction of disc herniation is posterolateral.

Herniated Nucleus Pulposus

As the posterior longitudinal ligament courses through the lumbar spine, it tends to get narrow at the base. This ligament prevents hyperflexion of the lumbar spine. It also serves as a reinforcement of the annulus. Because the ligament narrows at the lower lumbar spine, a weakness is created at the posteriolateral portion of the intervertebral disc. Such a weakness predisposes this area to herniation. Ninety-eight percent of herniations occur between L4 and L5 or between L5 and S1. **A herniated disc in the lumbar region will exert pressure on the nerve root of the vertebrae below. For example, a herniation between L5 and S1 will affect the nerve root of S1.** Pain will often originate from the lumbar spine and radiate down the leg into the foot. It is characterized as a sharp burning pain with almost an electric quality. On examination, the patient will have weakness of the affected myotome, decreased reflexes, and decreased sensation to the affected dermatome. Often there will be a positive straight leg raise test. Diagnosis can be made with clinical suspicion, EMG, or MRI. MRI is considered the gold standard.

Most cases can be treated conservatively with bed rest initially; oral pain medication and muscle relaxants are of value in the first few days. Initial OMT should be directed at myofascial structures. Gentle, indirect techniques are often the rule. Once the pain has lessened, more aggressive, direct type treatments can be employed. HVLA is relatively contraindicated in an acute herniated disc.

Clinical Correlate

Psoas Syndrome

- Patient position is flexed and sidebent to one side.

- Patient complains of inability to stand up straight.

- Nonneutral L1 or L2

- Nonneutral L5

- Backward sacral torsion

- Ipsilateral psoas muscle spasm

- Contralateral pelvic shift (away from psoas spasm)

- Contralateral piriformis muscle spasm (opposite from psoas spasm) with a same-sided pseudo-radiculopathy as the piriformis spasm

- Exaggerated lumbar lordosis in supine position

Flexion Contracture of the Iliopsoas (Psoas Syndrome)

Shortening or spasm of the iliopsoas muscle. This condition is usually initiated by positions that shorten the origin and insertion of the psoas muscle for some significant length of time. Sitting in a chair, bending over from the waist for a long period, getting up too quickly from a squatting position, and working at a desk are common precipitating events. Pain is often described as a dull ache in the low back; sometimes it refers to the groin. Other organic causes must be ruled out, including femoral bursitis, prostatitis, and salpingitis. On examination, the patient may have a tenderpoint at the iliacus muscle (medial to the ASIS). There may be a positive Thomas test. The key problem is the nonneutral dysfunction of L1 or L2.

Treatment depends upon the acuteness of the psoas spasm. Counterstrain works well at the iliacus and psoas. Ice also has been suggested as an initial treatment. If the syndrome is not too acute, manipulation to remove the key nonneutral dysfunction of the spine will cause the psoas syndrome to disappear. Some authors regard treating the nonneutral dysfunction at L1 or L2 as essential.

Spinal Stenosis

Osteoarthritis, osteophytes, bony depositions within ligaments, and hypertrophy of facet joints can all narrow the space around the spinal cord. If the space is narrowed enough (if it becomes stenosed), nerve impingement can occur. This condition is referred to as spinal stenosis. Pain may originate in the lower back and radiate down the leg. Leg symptoms include weakness, numbness, and pain. Pain is often worsened by standing, walking, or lying supine. On examination, the patient will usually have diminished reflexes, weakness in the affected myotomes (usually >1) and decreased sensation to the affected dermatomes (usually >1). Radiographs may reveal degenerative spondylosis, marked narrowing of the intervertebral disc and foramina, and osteophyte formation. Treatment includes patient education, NSAIDs, or low-dose rapidly tapering oral steroid. Pharmacologic measures have limited use. OMT should focus on myofascial structures, as well as bone alignment. Restoring symmetry and treating lumbar hyperlordosis may provide additional comfort. Avoid treatments that place the patient in the hyperlordotic position.

Spondylolisthesis

Spondylolisthesis occurs when one vertebral body slips in relation to the one below. This usually occurs between L5 and S1, and there is usually a defect in the region of the junction of the lamina with the pedicle (pars interarticularis). The condition may be asymptomatic or minimally symptomatic; however, patients may have back pain that radiates posteriorly to or below the knee. It is often worse with standing. True nerve compression symptoms are rare. On examination palpation of the lumbar spinous processes may reveal a "step off." Lateral radiographs will demonstrate the translation of one vertebra on the other. Flexion exercises and observation are indicated. Avoid activities that aggravate the condition. Patients with significant pain and or slippage >50% may require surgical fusion.

Spondylolysis

Spondylolysis is a defect in the pars interarticularis (often unilaterally) *without* anterior displacement of the vertebral body. Patients present as above, but with even milder symptoms. **Diagnosis can be made with oblique view of the lumbar spine. The fracture in the pars interarticularis is often described as a "collar on the Scotty dog."**

Cauda Equina Syndrome

A large, central disc herniation may compress the tail of the lumbar spine, causing a compression of the sacral nerve roots. The patient will present with pain similar to that of a herniated disc. However, because some sacral roots are impinged (S2–S4 control bowel and bladder infection), there will also be bowel and bladder dysfunction, decreased rectal tone, and saddle anesthesia. Emergent surgical decompression of the cauda equina is imperative. If surgery is delayed too long, irreversible paralysis may occur.

Table 4-1. Nerve Root Dysfunctions

Nerve Root	Motor	Sensory	Reflex
L4	Dorsiflexion of the foot (anterior tibialis)	Medial calf (medial malleolus)	Knee (patella)
L5	Dorsiflexion of big toe (extensor hallucis longus)	• Lateral calf • Dorsal foot/big toe	—
S1	Plantarflexion (peroneus longus and brevis gastrocnemius)	• Plantar section of foot • Lateral foot/malleolus	Achilles

Sacrum and Innominates 5

ANATOMY

Bones and Bony Landmarks

The innominate is composed of 3 fused bones: the ileum, the ischium, and the pubis bones. The sacrum is composed of 5 fused vertebrae.

Superior sulci, a.k.a. superior poles, are used for sacral static palpatory diagnosis. They are located ½ inch medial and ½ inch superior to the PSIS. Depending on the type of dysfunction, sulci are said to appear as shallow or deep, posterior or anterior. The ILAs are on the lateral edge of the distal aspect of the sacrum. Depending on the type of dysfunction, ILAs are said to appear as shallow or deep, posterior or anterior, cephalad, caudad.

COMLEX Note

Some will state that ILAs are landmarks to be used in superior inferior descriptions. Instead, use the term "inferior poles" to represent the shallow, deep, posterior, and anterior positions.

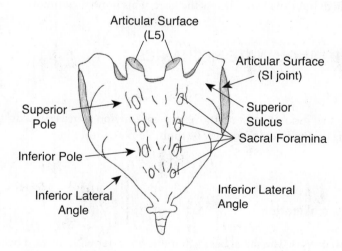

Figure 5-1. The Sacrum

Articulations

- **Acetabulum**
- **SI joint**—surrounded by strong, thick pelvic ligaments (anterior, posterior, and interosseouss sacroiliac ligaments). It is an L-shaped joint with an upper and lower arm. Somatic dysfunction can occur in either arm.
- **Pubic symphysis**

Ligaments

The **sacrotuberous ligament** originates from the ILA of the sacrum and inserts onto the ischial tuberosity. It forms the medial border of the greater sciatic foramen. It can be used as a tool for diagnosis of pelvic dysfunction (sacrum and innominate dysfunctions).

The **sacrospinous ligament** originates from the ischial spine and inserts onto the sacrum. This ligament divides the greater and lesser sciatic foramina.

The **sacroiliac ligaments** are anterior, posterior, and interosseous.

The **iliolumbar** originates from the transverse processes of L4 and L5 and inserts just superior to the PSIS. It is generally thought that these are the first ligaments to become painful in some low-back pain conditions.

Muscles

The **pelvic diaphragm** is composed of the levator ani (iliococcygeus and pubococcygeus muscles) and coccygeus muscles. The pelvic diaphragm moves in concert with the thoracoabdominal diaphragm to help return lymph back to the heart.

The **piriformis** originates at the anterior surface of the sacrum near the ILA and inserts onto the greater trochanter. Contraction of this muscle externally rotates the femur. Approximately 12% of the population will have the entire or peroneal portion of the sciatic nerve running through the belly of the piriformis. Therefore, piriformis hypertonicity can cause buttock pain that radiates down the thigh but usually not below the knee. This is more commonly known as sciatica.

SACRAL AND INNOMINATE MECHANICS

Innominates

Physiologically, the innominates rotate about an inferior transverse axis of the sacrum. However, during dysfunctions there may be multiple axes of rotation.

Sacrum

Four types of sacral motion

- **Postural motion:** The sacral base will move posterior with forward bending. The sacral base will move anterior with backward bending.
- **Respiratory motion:** During inhalation, the sacral base will move posterior. During exhalation, the sacral base will move anterior.
- **Inherent motion:** During craniosacral flexion, the sacrum extends or counternutates. During craniosacral extension, the sacrum flexes or nutates.
- **Dynamic motion:** motion that occurs during ambulation. The sacrum engages two sacral oblique axes. Weight bearing on the left leg (stepping forward with the right leg) will cause a left sacral axis to be engaged. The opposite is true for weight bearing on the right leg.

EVALUATION OF THE PELVIS AND INNOMINATES

Static Testing

Static testing examines certain anatomical landmarks without testing for motion. The purpose is to compare the 2 sides of each landmark for asymmetries, in particular asymmetries in height and depth.

Table 5-1

Posterior Landmarks	Anterior Landmarks
Posterior superior iliac spines (PSIS)	Anterior superior iliac spines (ASIS)
Gluteal folds	Iliac crests
Greater trochanters	Medial malleoli
Ischial tuberosity	
Sacral sulci	
Pubic tubercles	

Motion Testing

Standing Flexion Test—While the patient is standing, both thumbs are placed on the inferior aspects of the PSIS. The patient is asked to bend forward, which normally causes the PSIS to rise superiorly. A positive test results when one side is restricted, causing that PSIS to rise earlier and higher than the contralateral PSIS. **An iliosacral dysfunction exists on the same side as the positive test result.**

Seated Flexion Test—While the patient is sitting, both thumbs are placed on the inferior aspect of the PSIS. The patient is asked to bend forward, and the movement of the PSIS is noted. In the sitting position, the innominates are locked and thus any motion resulting is sacral. A positive test results when one side is restricted, causing that PSIS to rise earlier and higher than the contralateral PSIS. **A sacroiliac dysfunction exists on the same side as the positive test result.**

Innominate/Pelvic Rocking—A gentle and firm rocking motion against the ASIS with a posterior force. A positive test result is noted when there is resistance/restriction of one of the innominates against the rocking.

Interpretation

Innominates/Pubis—When evaluating the pelvis, the assessment of the ASIS and PSIS will describe the anatomical orientation of the innominates. If the innominates can be pictured as semi-circles, the position of the ASIS and PSIS help explain in which direction the half circle has moved. The clarification if one is moving forward in relation to the other, or vice versa, comes from the standing flexion test, which will clarify on which side the dysfunction is. The pubic tubercle assessment will clarify whether one is superior or inferior (shears) and the standing flexion test will clarify the side.

COMLEX Note

Traditionally, the Seated Flexion Test uses the PSIS of the innominate as a landmark; better results are obtained, however, if the superior poles of the sacrum are palpated as well during the test.

Sacrum—Interpreting the sacrum results can be confusing. The first area to assess is L5 (see later L5 rules). The seated flexion test is the next test to be done, which will clarify on which side the dysfunction is, **particularly which side of the sacrum has moved.** This is why even in a left-on-left torsion there is a positive seated flexion test on the right; the top right lateral aspect of the sacrum has rotated left on a left axis. If the sacrum can be pictured as a square and the sacral sulci as corners on that square, a deep sulcus can be interpreted as the square rotating away from that corner, and a shallow sulcus can be interpreted as the square moving toward that corner. The ILA gives the same information, but on a different part of the square.

SOMATIC DYSFUNCTION OF THE INNOMINATES AND SACRUM

Innominate Dysfunction

Anterior innominate rotation

Static findings:

- ASIS more inferior and medial ipsilaterally
- PSIS more superior and lateral ipsilaterally
- Longer leg ipsilaterally

Dynamic findings:

- AP compression restricted ipsilaterally
- Positive standing flexion test ipsilaterally

Posterior innominate rotation

Static findings:

- ASIS more superior and lateral ipsilaterally
- PSIS more inferior and medial ipsilaterally
- Shorter leg ipsilaterally

Dynamic findings:

- AP compression restricted ipsilaterally
- Positive standing flexion test ipsilaterally

Superior innominate shear (upslip, superior innominate subluxation)

Static findings:

- ASIS and PSIS more superior ipsilaterally
- Pubic rami may be superior ipsilaterally

Dynamic findings:

- AP compression restricted ipsilaterally
- Positive standing flexion test ipsilaterally

COMLEX Note

Recommended Innominate Evaluation Sequence

1. Standing flexion test
2. Static landmark findings
3. Iliosacral motion
4. Leg length

Inferior innominate shear
(innominate downslip inferior innominate subluxation)

Static findings:

- ASIS and PSIS more inferior ipsilaterally

Dynamic findings:

- AP compression restricted ipsilaterally
- Positive standing flexion test ipsilaterally

Outflare

Static findings:

- ASIS more lateral ipsilaterally
- PSIS more medial ipsilaterally
- Leg externally rotated ipsilaterally
- Increased distance from umbilicus

Dynamic findings:

- Lateral to medial compression restricted ipsilaterally
- Positive standing flexion test ipsilaterally

Inflare

Static findings:

- ASIS more medial ipsilaterally
- PSIS more lateral ipsilaterally
- Leg internally rotated ipsilaterally
- Decreased distance from umbilicus

Dynamic findings:

- Medial to lateral motion restricted ipsilaterally
- Positive standing flexion test ipsilaterally

Gapped pubes

Static findings:

- Palpable gap at pubic symphysis
- Usually tender

Compressed pubes

Static findings:

- Bulge at pubic symphysis
- Usually tender

Superior pubic shear

Static findings:

- Pubic tubercle superiorly ipsilaterally
- Positive standing flexion test ipsilaterally

Inferior pubic shear

Static findings:

- AP compression restricted ipsilaterally
- Pubic tubercle inferiorly ipsilaterally
- Positive standing flexion test ipsilaterally

Sacral Somatic Dysfunction

Sacral torsions

Sacral rotation occurs about an oblique axis, often along with somatic dysfunction at L5.

Sacral torsion rules:

Rule 1: When L5 is sidebent, a sacral oblique axis is engaged on the same side as the sidebending.

Rule 2: When L5 is rotated, the sacrum rotates the opposite way on an oblique axis.

Rule 3: The seated flexion test is found to be positive on the opposite side of the oblique axis.

Forward sacral torsion

In a forward sacral torsion, rotation is on the same side of the axis.

Left rotation on a left oblique axis (L on L). Left rotation occurs as the right superior sulcus moves anterior while the left ILA moves posterior.

- Right superior sulcus deeper
- Left ILA shallow
- Positive seated flexion test on the *right*
- Restricted springing on the left ILA
- L5 ($NS_L R_R$)
- Sphinx or lumbar extension test improves/lessens superior sulcus asymmetry
- Abnormal sacral rock

Right rotation on a right oblique axis (R on R). Right rotation occurs as the left superior sulcus moves anterior while the left ILA moves posterior.

- Left superior sulcus deeper
- Right ILA shallow
- Positive seated flexion test on the *left*
- Restricted springing on the right ILA
- L5 ($NS_R R_L$)
- Sphinx or lumbar extension test improves/lessens superior sulcus asymmetry
- Abnormal sacral rock

COMLEX Note

An anterior sacrum dysfunction is like an anterior torsion, and a posterior sacrum dysfunction is like a posterior torsion. The only exception is that **L5** does not behave as would be expected in the torsions.

COMLEX Note

- Forward sacral torsions are also called physiologic torsions.
- Backward sacral torsions are also called nonphysiologic torsions.

Backward sacral torsion

Right rotation on a left oblique axis (R on L). Right rotation occurs as the right superior sulcus moves posterior and the left ILA moves anterior.

- Right superior sulcus shallow
- Left ILA deeper
- Positive seated flexion test on the *right*
- Positive lumbosacral spring test
- Restricted springing on the right superior sulcus
- L5 (NNR_LS_L)
- Sphinx or lumbar extension test worsens/increases superior sulcus asymmetry
- Abnormal sacral rock

Left rotation on a right oblique axis (L on R). Left rotation occurs as the left superior sulcus moves posterior and the right ILA moves anterior.

- Left superior sulcus shallow
- Right ILA deeper
- Positive seated flexion test on the *left*
- Positive lumbosacral spring test
- Restricted springing on the left superior sulcus
- L5 (NNR_RS_R)
- Sphinx or lumbar extension test worsens/increases superior sulcus asymmetry
- Abnormal sacral rock

COMLEX Note

85% of forward sacral torsions are L on L, while 85% of backward sacral torsions are L on R.

Bilateral sacral flexion (sacral base anterior)

- Right and left superior sulci deep
- Increased lumbar curve
- ILAs shallow bilaterally
- Restricted springing on ILAs bilaterally
- *False* negative seated flexion test
- Abnormal sacral rock

Bilateral sacral extensions (sacral base posterior)

- Right and left superior sulci shallow
- Decreased lumbar curve
- ILAs deeper bilaterally
- Positive lumbosacral spring test
- Restricted springing on superior sulci bilaterally
- *False* negative seated flexion test
- Abnormal sacral rock

Sacral shears (unilateral sacral flexion/extension [USF/USE])

In this somatic dysfunction, the sacrum will shift anteriorly or posteriorly around a transverse axis.

In a unilateral sacral flexion on the right (USFR), the sacral base will shift anterior on the right.

- Right superior sulcus deep
- Positive seated flexion test on the right
- Abnormal sacral rock

In a unilateral sacral extension on the right (USER), the sacral base will shift posterior on the right.

- Right superior sulcus shallow
- Positive seated flexion test on the right
- Abnormal sacral rock

Recommended Sacral Evaluation Sequence

1. Seated flexion test

2. Sacroiliac motion assessment and/or sacral rock assessment

3. Four-corner assessment (superior and inferior poles) + ILAs

4. Springing and/or lumbar extension (sphinx) test

COMLEX Note

In sacral shears, a key diagnostic feature is that the ILAs will appear unlevel in a cephalad/caudad orientation.

SHOULDER

COMLEX Note

- Know the landmarks of the shoulder.

- Know where the names of arteries change.

- Know the muscles and their actions.

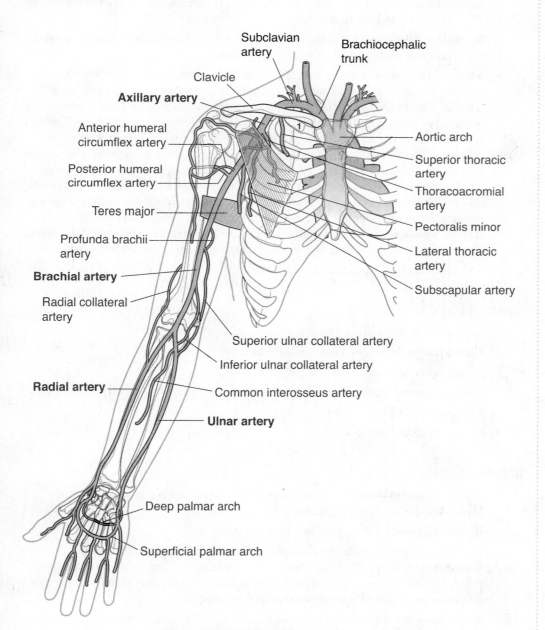

Subclavian artery

Brachiocephalic trunk

Clavicle

Axillary artery

Anterior humeral circumflex artery

Posterior humeral circumflex artery

Teres major

Profunda brachii artery

Brachial artery

Radial collateral artery

Aortic arch

Superior thoracic artery

Thoracoacromial artery

Pectoralis minor

Lateral thoracic artery

Subscapular artery

Superior ulnar collateral artery

Inferior ulnar collateral artery

Radial artery

Common interosseus artery

Ulnar artery

Deep palmar arch

Superficial palmar arch

Figure 6-1. The Shoulder

Anatomy

Bones

- **Clavicle**—acts as a strut to prevent shoulder from compressing neurovascular structures in axilla.
- **Scapula**—contains glenoid fossa (socket) of shoulder, coracoid process; acromion, which articulates with clavicle.
- **Humerus**

Joints

COMLEX Note

Normally, there should be a 2:1 ratio of motion between the glenohumeral joint and the scapulothoracic joint.

COMLEX Note

Know the difference between a dislocated shoulder and a separated shoulder.

- **Scapulothoracic**—approximately 60° of motion is available by the scapula moving in relation to the posterior thorax.
- **Sternoclavicular**—located at the top of the sternum. This joint may become sprained with clavicular displacement in relation to sternum.
- **Acromioclavicular**—provides fore/aft, anterior/posterior, and superior/inferior motion. The clavicle may become restricted in relation to the acromion process of the scapula. The clavicle rotates about a long axis down the shaft of the bone. Dysfunction is named in relation to the acromion. To diagnose clavicular motion at the A/C joint, place one finger on the acromion and one on the distal clavicle. Bring the arm into extension. You should feel the free edge of the clavicle become prominent. Then, move the arm into flexion. The free edge of the distal clavicle should be less prominent or flat. If the free edge stays prominent when you move the arm into flexion, it is termed an anterior clavicle (the clavicle is anterior in relation to the acromion). If the free edge remains flat as you bring the arm into extension, it is termed a posterior clavicle (the clavicle is posterior in relation to the acromion). OMT treatment involves holding the clavicle and moving the acromion to meet the clavicle, using the humerus as a lever.
- **Glenohumeral**—is the actual shoulder joint.

Ligaments

- Capsule, with thickenings
- Glenoid labrum (forms an elevated edge to the glenoid fossa)
- Muscle tendons (rotator cuff, biceps, triceps)
- Coraco-humeral ligament
- Clavicular ligaments
- Coracoacromial ligament

Muscles: trunk to scapula

- **Serratus anterior**—attaches from antero-lateral ribs to medial border of scapula. Moves scapula anteriorly or medially.
- **Rhomboids**—attaches scapula to midline of spine
- **Levator**—elevates scapula. Attaches at upper medial border of scapula to posterior tubercles of cervicals. The attachment at the upper medial border is a counterstrain point, a myofascial trigger point, a fibromyalgia tender point, etc. Tenderness at this point can be a trigger for an upper thoracic/rib complex.
- **Trapezius**—this large muscle is the most superficial. The general investing fascia splits to incorporate the trapezius and the sternocleidomastoid. The upper trapezius elevates

the scapula, the lower trapezius depresses the scapula. During the process of lifting with the upper limb, the trapezius provides a muscular connection between the scapula and the trunk/neck.

- **Pectoralis minor**—attaches from the coracoid process to the upper ribs (ribs 3–5). Painful shoulders are frequently protracted and the pectoralis minor is tight. (*Note:* Pectoralis major attaches to the humerus.)
- **Rotator cuff** (mnemonic: SITS)
  - S = supraspinatus (abduction of the arm)
  - I = infraspinatus (external rotation of arm)
  - T = teres minor (external rotation of arm)
  - S = subscapulais (internal rotation of arm)

Table 6-1. Summary of Muscle Actions

Abduction	supraspinatus, deltoid
Adduction	pectoralis major, latissimus dorsi
Flexion	coracobrachialis, anterior portion of deltoid
Extension	latissimus dorsi, teres major, posterior deltoid
External rotation	infraspinatus, teres minor
Internal rotation	subscapularis, pectoralis major, teres major, and latissimus dorsi

Arterial supply

- The **subclavian artery** passes between the anterior and middle scalenes. The subclavian vein passes anterior to the anterior scalene. Therefore, contracture of the anterior and middle scalenes may compromise arterial supply to the arm but may not affect venous drainage.
- The **radial artery** courses the lateral aspect of the forearm supplying blood to the elbow, wrist, dorsal aspect of the hand, and eventually forming most of the deep palmar arterial arch.
- The **ulnar artery** courses the medial aspect of the forearm supplying blood to the elbow, wrist, dorsal aspect of the hand, and eventually forming most of the superficial palmar arterial arch.

Lymphatic drainage of the upper extremities

- Right upper extremity drains into the right subclavian duct.
- Left upper extremity drains into the thoracic duct.

Nerves

The brachial plexus is responsible for supplying the nerves to the upper extremity. It is composed of nerves from roots C5–C8 and T1 (*see* Table 6-2).

COMLEX Note
- Know the rotator cuff muscles.
- Know the pectoralis minor muscle origin and insertion.

COMLEX Note
The most commonly injured rotator cuff muscle is the supraspinatus.

Clinical Correlate
- A drop-arm test will be positive in someone who has a supraspinatus tear or weakness.
- A positive apprehension test may indicate a shoulder that may easily dislocate or a bicep tendon that is irritated.

COMLEX Note
Memorize the brachial plexus nerve roots and lesions.

Table 6-2

Nerve Root	Sensation	Motor	Reflex
C5	Lateral arm and lateral aspect of elbow	Deltoid and biceps	Biceps reflex
C6	Lateral forearm and thumb	Biceps and wrist extensors	Brachioradialis reflex
C7	Middle finger	Triceps and wrist flexors	Triceps reflex
C8	Little finger and middle forearm	Wrist flexors and interossi	None
T1	Medial elbow and medial arm	Interossi	None

COMLEX Note

Know that a <2 to 1 ratio can be used to describe a frozen shoulder, rather than giving the abduction of the arm in degrees.

Motion Testing and Examination of the Shoulder

Normally, the arm can abduct to 180° with active motion: 120° is due to glenohumeral motion, and 60° is due to scapulothoracic motion. *Therefore, for every 3° of abduction, the glenohumeral joint moves 2°, and the scapulothoracic joint moves 1°.*

Motion testing of the shoulder

Apley Scratch Test—used to evaluate for the active range of motion of the shoulder. The purpose of the test is to have the patient reach the scapula opposite of the shoulder the physician is testing from various angles. The angles are: across the patient's chest, behind the patient's back, and over the patient's head. This test assess the full range of motion of the shoulder joint.

Arm Drop Test—used to evaluate for a possible rotator cuff tear. The patient abducts his/her arm to 90°. If there is a full tear of the rotator cuff, the patient will be unable to hold the arm up and the arm will drop. To test for a possible partial tear, the physician applies a downward tap on the arm. If there is a partial tear, the arm will drop as well.

Apprehension Test—for chronic shoulder dislocation. The patient's shoulder is abducted, extended, and externally rotated. The patient should perceive the oncoming dislocation and become uncomfortable or apprehensive (hence the test's name).

Yergason Test—used to assess the stability of the biceps tendon in the humeral bicipital groove. Traction is applied to the patient's elbow followed by external rotation. At this point, the patient is instructed to actively internally rotate against the resistance of the physician. A positive test results in the tendon popping out of the groove with some discomfort for the patient. This test is consistent with an unstable tendon and can lead to bicipital tendonitis and/or tenosynovitis.

Adson's Test—used to assess for thoracic outlet syndrome. The patient has his/her shoulder extended, externally rotated, and mildly abducted. The elbow is extended as well, and the patient's radial pulse is monitored. Then, the patient is asked to turn his/her head toward the same side being tested and to take a deep breath. A positive test when there is a decreased or absent radial pulse.

Neurologic Examination of the Upper Extremity

A basic neurologic exam will evaluate muscle strength, sensation, and deep tendon reflexes.

Deep tendon reflex evaluation

Although differences may be subtle, Table 6-3 shows the standard way to record the amplitude of a reflex.

Table 6-3

Grade	Definition
4/4	Brisk with sustained clonus
3/4	Brisk with unsustained clonus
2/4	Normal
1/4	Decreased but present
0/4	Absent

Muscle strength recording

Table 6-4 shows the standard method for recording motor strength.

Table 6-4

Grade	Diagnosis	Definition
5	Normal	Full range of motion (FROM) against gravity and full resistance
4	Good	FROM against gravity with some resistance
3	Fair	FROM against gravity with no resistance
2	Poor	FROM with gravity eliminated
1	Trace	Evidence of slight contractility
0	Zero	No evidence of contractility

Common Problems of the Shoulder

Thoracic outlet syndrome

- **Pathogenesis**—compression of the neurovascular bundle (subclavian artery and vein, and the brachial plexus). Compression can occur in 6 places:
  1. Nerve root avulsion
  2. Cervical rib
  3. Between anterior and middle scalene
  4. Between first rib and clavicle
  5. Between pectoralis minor and upper ribs
  6. Pancoast tumor
- **Location of pain**—neck pain or pain radiating to arm
- **Quality of pain**—ache or parasthesias

- **Signs and symptoms**—On examination, the scalenes, a cervical rib, or the clavicle may be tender. Often there is a positive Adson's, Roos, or hyperabduction test.
- **Treatment**—OMT should be directed at improving restriction usually found in the cervical region, thoracic inlet, clavicle, scalene, and surrounding musculature.

Supraspinatus tendonitis

- **Pathogenesis**—continuous impingement of the greater tuberosity against the acromion as the arm is flexed and internally rotated
- **Location of pain**—tenderness, especially at the tip of the acromion
- **Signs and symptoms**—The pain is usually exacerbated by abduction, especially from 60° to 120°. This is commonly referred to as the "painful arc." A positive drop arm test is a common sign.
- **Treatment**—Rest, ice, and NSAIDs for the acute stages. OMT should be directed at the shoulder complex, upper thoracic, and ribs to free up motion and loosen the fascia of the shoulder girdle to expedite the healing process.

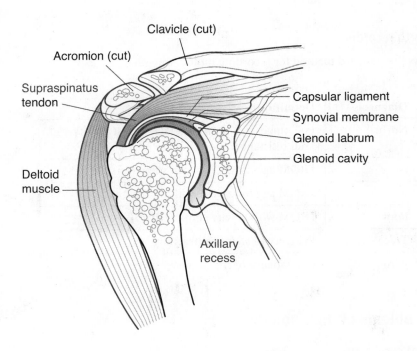

Figure 6-2. Supraspinatus Tendon

Rotator cuff tear

- **Definition**—a tear at the insertion of one of the rotator cuff tendons, usually the supraspinatus
- **Etiology**—often associated with trauma
- **Location of pain**—tenderness just below the tip of the acromion
- **Quality of pain**—a transient sharp pain in the shoulder followed by a steady ache that may last for days

- **Signs and symptoms**—In minor supraspinatus tears, a weakness in active abduction is often present, along with a positive drop arm test. Atrophy is a common sign.
- **Treatment**—OMT should be directed at freeing up any restrictions in the glenohumeral area, as well as treating the clavicle, upper thoracic, and ribs for somatic dysfunction.

Bicipital tenosynovitis

- **Pathogenesis**—an inflammation of the tendon and sheath of the long head of the biceps, leading to adhesions that bind the tendon to the bicipital groove. It also may result from a subluxation of the bicipital tendon out of the bicipital groove.
- **Location of pain**—anterior portion of the shoulder
- **Signs and symptoms**—Tenderness is usually present over the bicipital groove.
- **Treatment**—OMT should include freeing up any restrictions in the glenohumeral area, as well as myofascial release.

Adhesive capsulitis/frozen shoulder syndrome

- **Definition**—a common condition characterized by pain and restriction of shoulder motion that increasingly gets worse over the course of one year
- **Signs and symptoms**—decreased range of motion
- **Epidemiology**—most often seen in patients over 40
- **Etiology**—caused by prolonged immobility of the shoulder
- **Location of pain**—Tenderness is usually at the anterior portion of the shoulder.
- **Treatment**—The main goal is prevention. Early mobilization following shoulder injury is essential. OMT should be directed at improving motion and lysing adhesions.

Winging of the scapula

A weakness of the anterior serratus muscle usually due to a long thoracic nerve injury

Brachial plexus injuries

Erb-Duchenne's palsy is by far the most common form of brachial plexus injury. It is an upper arm paralysis caused by injury to C5 and C6 nerve roots usually during childbirth (shoulder dystocia).

ELBOW, WRIST, AND HAND

Anatomy

Bones

- **Radius**
- **Ulna**
- **Eight carpal bones**
    - Scaphoid
    - Lunate
    - Triquetral

> **Clinical Correlate**
>
> **Erb-Duchenne's palsy** will cause a "waiter's tip" presentation of the arm. The arm will hang straight down, with a slight internal rotation, and the wrist will be flexed.

> **COMLEX Note**
>
> The **pronator teres muscle** may cause entrapment of the median nerve in the forearm.

COMLEX Note

Scaphoid is the most common fractured carpal bone, while the lunate is the most common dislocated carpal bone.

Pisiform

Trapezium

Trapezoid

Capitate

Hamate

- **Five metacarpals**
- **Fourteen phalanges**

Joints

- Elbow (ulna and humerus)
- Ulna and radial (distal and proximal)
- Intercarpals, carpometacarpals, metacarpophalangeal (MCP), and interphalangeal (PIP and DIP)

Muscles and innervations

- Primary **flexors of the wrist and hand**, most of which are innervated by the median nerve (except for flexor carpi ulnaris [ulnar nerve])
- Primary **extensors of the wrist and hand** originate at the lateral epicondyle of the humerus, all of which are innervated by the radial nerve.
- Primary **supinators** of the forearm are the biceps (musculocutaneous nerve) and the supinator (radial nerve).
- Primary **pronators** of the forearm are the pronator teres and pronator quadratus (radial nerve).

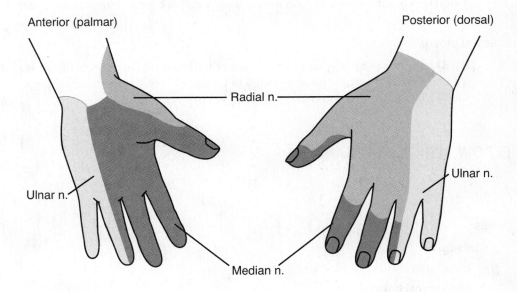

Figure 6-3. Hand Innervation

Muscles of the hand

- Thenar eminence is innervated by the median nerve (except for adductor pollicis brevis [ulnar nerve]).
- Hypothenar eminence and interossi are innervated by the ulnar nerve.
- Lumbricles (four)

    First and second lumbricles are innervated by the median nerve.

    Third and fourth lumbricles are innervated by the ulnar nerve.

Motion of the Elbow and Forearm

Carrying angle (*see* Figure 6-4)

- Formed by the intersection of two lines. The first line is the longitudinal axis of the humerus. The second line starts at the distal ulnar radial joint and passes through the proximal radial ulna joint.
- A carrying angle >15° is called cubitus valgus or *abduction of the ulna* if somatic dysfunction is present.
- A carrying angle <3° is called cubitis varus or *adduction of the ulna* if somatic dysfunction is present.
- The carrying angle has a direct influence on the position of the wrist. Due to a parallelogram effect, *an increase in the carrying angle (abduction of the ulna) will cause an adduction of the wrist. Conversely, a decrease in the carrying angle (adduction of the ulna) will cause an abduction of the wrist.*

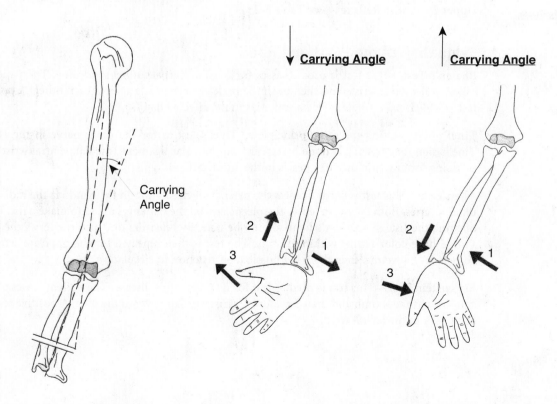

Figure 6-4 (*left*). The angle formed between the two dotted lines represents the carrying angle. **Figure 6-5** (*center*). Adduction of the ulna (*arrow #1*) will cause the radius to be pulled proximal (*arrow #2*). This will result in abduction of the wrist (*arrow #3*). **Figure 6-6** (*right*). Abduction of the ulna (*arrow #1*) will cause the radius to be pushed distal (*arrow #2*). This will result in adduction of the wrist (*arrow #3*).

Table 6-5

Carrying Angle	Ulna Movement	Wrist Movement
Decreased	Adduction	Abduction
Increased	Abduction	Adduction

Radial head motion

When the forearm is pronated, the radial head will glide posteriorly. When the forearm is supinated, the radial head will glide anteriorly.

Evaluation of the Elbow

Tinel Test—The space between the medial epicondyle and olecranon is found and tapped on by the physician. Marked pain or tingling in the region or distal to the region may indicate irritation or compression of the ulnar nerve.

Tennis Elbow Test (Golf Elbow Test)—The patient is instructed to make a fist and extend his/her wrist. The patient then actively resists the physician pushing against the dorsum of the patient's hand. A positive test will elicit pain on the lateral epicondyle.

Valgus/Varus Strain—This test is done to assess for stability of the ligaments of the elbow. A valgus stress (away from the body) and then a varus stress (toward the body) is placed on the elbow, which is assessed for laxity.

Upper Extremity Reflexes—*see* Table 6-2

COMLEX Note

Know the difference between Tinel test and Tinel sign

Evaluation of the Wrist and Hand

Phalen's Test—This test is used to asses for possible carpal tunnel syndrome. The patient is asked to flex both wrists and then push the back of both hands against each other. A positive test will elicit pain, tingling, or paresthesias in the affected hand.

Tinel's Sign—Using the same principle as Tinel's test as for the ulnar nerve in the elbow, Tinel's sign for the wrist is done by tapping on the volar ligament (medial, ventral wrist) and assessing for any pain or paresthesias in the affected hand.

Allen Test—This test is used to assess the patency of circulation in the hand via the radial and ulnar arteries. Both are occluded by the physician and the patient is asked to make a fist. Upon opening the fist, the patient's hand should be pale. By releasing one of the arteries the hand should have color return within seconds. The test is then repeated for the opposite artery. If color does not return then there is a possible obstruction to circulation.

Finkelstein Test—This test is used to test for de Quervain's disease. The patient closes all fingers around the thumb and then deviates the wrist medially toward the ulna. A positive test will elicit pain in the lateral wrist.

Somatic Dysfunction of the Forearm

Adduction of the ulna

See Figure 6-5.

Abduction of the ulna

See Figure 6-6.

Posterior radial head

- Falling on a pronated forearm is often a common cause.
- Restricted in supination, freedom toward pronation
- Radial head more dorsum/posterior

Anterior radial head

- Falling on a supinated forearm is often a common cause.
- Restricted in pronation, freedom toward supination
- Radial head more ventral/anterior

Common Complaints of the Forearm and Wrist

Carpal tunnel syndrome

- **Definition**—Collection of signs and symptoms which occurs after compression of the median nerve within the carpal tunnel
- **Quality and location of pain**—Patient usually complains of paresthesias on the palmar surface of the thumb and the first 2 ½ digits.
- **Signs and symptoms**—Weakness and atrophy usually appear late. On examination, symptoms are reproduced with Tinel's, phalen, and prayer tests.
- **Treatment**—usually consists of splints, NSAIDs, and steroid injections. Surgery is indicated if medical treatment has failed. OMT is usually very helpful and should be directed at correcting upper thoracic and rib dysfunctions, decreasing sympathetic tone in the upper extremity, and removing any myofascial restrictions.

Lateral epicondylitis (tennis elbow)

- **Definition**—a strain of the extensor muscles of the forearm near the lateral epicondyle
- **Location of pain**—The patient usually complains of pain over the lateral epicondyle that worsens with supination against resistance.
- **Signs and symptoms**—Tenderness at the lateral epicondyle or just distal to it. Pain often worsens with activity.
- **Treatment**—NSAIDs, rest, and ice. OMT should be directed toward correcting cervical or upper thoracic dysfunctions, counterstrain to affected muscles (usually extensors), and myofascial release to decrease fascial restrictions.

Clinical Correlate

Any tenderness at the floor of the "anatomic snuff box" of the wrist indicates a possible fracture. It is most often the scaphoid, which is also at risk for avascular necrosis.

Medial epicondylitis (golfer's elbow)

- **Definition**—a strain of the flexor muscles of the forearm near the medial epicondyle
- **Quality and location of pain, signs and symptoms, treatment**—same for tennis elbow but directed at the medial epicondyle

Table 6-6. Upper Extremity Neuropathies

Nerve Damaged and Location	Finding	Description	Injury Mechanism
Median *n.* at wrist	Ape hand	• Thenar-wasting, adducted thumb, loss of thumb opposition	• Carpal tunnel syndrome
Median *n.* at forearm	Hand of Benediction noted when attempting to make a fist	• Deficits described above for median *n.* injury at wrist may be present • Flexion of PIP is lost in digits 2 and 3, and weakened in digits 4 and 5 • When making fist, digits 2 and 3 remain partially extended	• Pronator syndrome
Ulnar *n.* at elbow, wrist	Claw hand	• Contracture of digits 4 and 5 in MCP extension with flexion of PIP & DIP hypothenar atrophy • Clawing appearance is worse with ulnar nerve injury at wrist (tunnel of Guyon) than with injury at elbow (ulnar paradox)	• Medial epicondyle fracture or dislocation • Cubital tunnel syndrome (compression between 2 heads of flexor carpi ulnaris) • Guyon's tunnel compression
Radial *n.* at arm	Wrist drop (Saturday night palsy)	• Paralysis of wrist extensors	• Hanging arm over chair • Fracture of humerus at radial groove
Erb-Duchenn (upper trunk; C5, C6 roots of brachial plexus)	Waiter's tip	• Arm hangs at side in medial rotation, forearm is extended and pronated • Cannot abduct arm	• Shoulder dystocia • Fall on shoulder
Klumpke's palsy (lower trunk; C8, T1 roots of brachial plexus)	Claw hand	• Extension of MCP of digits 4 and 5 with flexion of PIP and DIP • C8/T1 dermatome numbness • May have Horner's syndrome (T1)	• Outstretch arm over head with extension

Lower Extremities

7

HIP AND KNEE

Anatomy

Bones and bony landmarks

- Femur
- Patella
- Tibia
- Fibula

Muscles of the hip and knee

- Hip

    Primary extensor—gluteus maximus

    Primary flexor—iliopsoas

- Knee

    Primary extensor—quadriceps

    Primary flexors—semimembranosis and semitendinosis

Ligaments and joints

- Hip

    Femoroacetabular joint (hip joint)

    - Iliofemoral ligament
    - Ischiofemoral ligament
    - Pubofemoral ligament
    - Capitis femoris

- Knee

Tibiofemoral joint

- **Anterior cruciate ligament** (ACL)—arises from the anterior part of the intercondylar area of the tibia, just posterior to the attachment of the medial meniscus. It extends superiorly, posteriorly, and laterally to attach to the posterior part of the medial side of the lateral condyle of the femur. It prevents posterior displacement of the femur on the tibia and hyperextension of the knee.
- **Posterior cruciate ligament** (PCL)—arises from the posterior part of the intercondylar area of the tibia and passes superiorly and anteriorly on the medial side of the anterior cruciate ligament to attach to the anterior part of the lateral

COMLEX Note

- Know the muscles and their actions.

- Know the common mechanisms of injury and the structures that are injured.

- Know the common orthopedic assessments.

surface of the medial condyle of the femur. It prevents anterior displacement of the femur and hyperflexion of the knee.

Lateral stabilizers of the knee

- **Medial collateral ligament** (tibial collateral ligament)—extends from the medial epicondyle of the femur to the medial condyle and superior part of the medial surface of the tibia. The deep fibers attach firmly to the medial meniscus.
- **Lateral collateral ligament** (fibular collateral ligament)—extends inferiorly from the lateral epicondyle of the femur to the lateral surface of the head of the fibula.

Patellofemoral joint

- The patella, a sesamoid bone, glides along the femoral condyles.

Tibiofibular joint

- The fibular head will glide anteriorly with pronation (dorsiflexion, eversion, and external rotation) of the foot.
- The fibular head will glide posteriorly with supination (plantar flexion, inversion, and internal rotation) of the foot.

Nerves

Femoral nerve (L2–L4)

- Motor—quadriceps, iliacus, sartorius, and pectineus
- Sensory—anterior thigh and medial leg

Sciatic nerve (L4–S3)

Two divisions:

Tibial

- Motor—hamstrings except short head of the biceps femoris, most plantar flexors, and toe flexors
- Sensory—lower leg and plantar aspect of foot

Peroneal

- Motor—short head of biceps femoris, evertors and dorsiflexors of the foot, and most extensors of the toes
- Sensory—lower leg and dorsum of foot

COMLEX Note

Dorsiflexion, eversion, and abduction = pronation of the ankle

Plantar flexion, inversion, and adduction = supination of the ankle

COMLEX Note

Short head of the biceps femoris is innervated by the common peroneal nerve.

Evaluation of the Hip

Patrick (FABERE) test is used to assess the range of motion of the hip. The patient is lying supine with the physician standing on the side to be tested. The physician grasps the patient's knee and ankle, and passively moves the knee and hip in the following motions:

- Complete flexion of the hip and knee (**F**lexion)
- Abduction of the knee with foot remaining in line with the opposite knee (**AB**duction)
- Once the knee is fully abducted, external rotation is added to bring leg into the anatomic barrier (**E**xternal **R**otation)
- Finally, the knee is pushed toward table, producing extension (**E**xtension)

Symmetry of motion should be noted. A positive test may illicit pain. If hard resistance is noticed, this may indicate bony obstruction of the motion of the hip (i.e., arthritis); if "soft" resistance is noticed, this may indicate muscular involvement (i.e., contractions, spasms). Pain elicited should be localized for further evaluation.

Ober test is used to assess for contracture of the tensor fascia lata/iliotibial band. The patient is lying on his/her side. The top most leg is flexed at the knee and lifted toward the ceiling. The leg is then released to fall. Normally it should fall quickly; if there is a delay or slow drop, this may indicate a contracture of the tensor fascia lata.

Ortolani's sign is used to assess congenital dysplasia or dislocation of the hip. It is usually performed on newborns. The patient's knees and hips are carefully flexed, and then the thighs are externally rotated and abducted. A positive test elicits a click.

Thomas test is used to assess for psoas contraction. While lying supine on the exam table, the patient is asked to flex both hips and knees and to use his/her arms to hug both legs and bring them as close to the patient's chest as possible. The patient then releases one leg, allowing it to fall on the table. The physician can exaggerate the extended leg by pushing the knee toward the table. At this point, the physician places a hand under the lumbar region to assess the extent of the lordosis and under the extended knee to assess the distance from the table. The procedure is then repeated for the other side. An exaggerated lumbar lordosis or distance of the knee from the table may indicate a psoas contraction or spasm, depending on the height difference.

Trendelenburg test is used to assess for a weak gluteus medius, or dislocation of the hip. The patient is asked to stand in front of the physician. Then the patient is asked to lift one leg of the floor. The physician is observing the position of the iliac crests from behind. Normally, the gluteus medius contracts when there is a weight change of the hip. In a normal patient, the iliac crests should remain at the same level, or with a slight rise on the side with the lifted leg. In a positive test, the side of the standing leg has a dramatic rise of the iliac crest, with the lifted side having a dramatic drop. There is also sidebending of the lumbar spine toward the lifted leg.

Erichsen's test is used to assess for possible sacroileitis. The patient is lying supine on the exam table. The physician applies bilateral medial pressure on the patient's pelvis. A positive test will elicit pain.

Straight leg test is used to assess for radiculopathy. The patient is lying supine on the exam table. The physician grasps the patient's ankle and extends the knee while raising the hip toward the ceiling. At the same time, the physician is assessing the ASIS with the other hand. A positive test elicits pain down the posterior aspect of the raised leg. Bending or bowing of the knee indicates contracture of the hamstrings.

Neurologic Evaluation

Table 7-1

Nerve Root	Motor	Reflex	Sensation
L1	Iliopsoas	None	Anterior thigh just below inguinal ligament
L2	Iliopsoas, adductors, quadriceps	None	Middle anterior thigh
L3	Adductors, quadriceps	None	Anterior thigh just above knee
L4	Anterior tibialis	Patella reflex	Medial malleolus
L5	Extensor hallicus longus, quadriceps	None	Dorsal aspect of foot and big toe
S1	Peroneus longus and brevis gastrocnemius	Achilles reflex	Lateral malleolus

Anatomic Variations and Q Angle (Quadriceps Angle)

The **normal angle** between the neck and shaft of the femur is 120–135°.

- If angle <120°, condition is coxa vara
- If angle >135°, condition is coxa valga

The **Q angle** is formed by the intersection of a line from the ASIS through the middle of the patella and a line from the tibial tubercle through the middle of the patella. An increased Q angle is referred to as genu valgum. A decreased Q angle is referred to as genu varum.

Somatic Dysfunction of the Fibular Head

Two somatic dysfunctions are possible with fibular head movement:

- **Posterior fibular head** is present when there is a restriction in anterior glide. The foot will appear more supinated when compared with the other side. The fibular head will resist any anterior springing.
- **Anterior fibular head** is present when there is a restriction in posterior glide. The foot will appear more pronated when compared with the other side. The fibular head will resist any posterior springing.

Clinical Considerations of the Hip and Knee

Lateral femoral patella tracking syndrome

An increased Q angle often causes an imbalance of the musculature of the quadriceps (strong vastus lateralis and weak vastus medialis). This imbalance will cause the patella to deviate laterally and will eventually lead to irregular or accelerated wearing on the posterior surface of the patella.

Often patients will complain of deep knee pain, especially when climbing stairs. The physician may notice atrophy in the vastus medialis, and often the patient will have a positive "grind test." Treatment is geared toward strengthening the vastus medialis muscle.

COMLEX Note

The common fibular nerve (a.k.a. common peroneal nerve) lies directly posterior to the proximal fibular head. Therefore, a posterior fibular head or fracture of the fibula may disturb the function of the common fibular nerve.

O'Donahue's triad (a.k.a. "unhappy triad," "terrible triad") is an injury to the ACL, medial meniscus, and medial collateral ligament. It is usually due to a posterior lateral force at the knee.

Compartment syndrome

The anterior compartment is most often affected, often resulting in severe unrelenting pain after and during exercise. The anterior tibialis muscle is hard and tender to palpation, and pulses are present; however, muscle strength may be diminished. Treatment usually consists of ice and myofascial release to increase venous and lymph return. If intracompartmental pressure is too great where arterial supply is reduced, a surgical fasciotomy must be done immediately.

Short leg syndrome

This clinical phenomenon is usually caused by a congenital defect in the growth and development of one lower extremity in comparison to the other, and is primarily associated with sacral base unleveling. The gold standard for diagnosis is standing postural x-ray of the pelvis to measure for sacral base unleveling. Treatment requires insertion of a heel lift into the shoe of the shortened lower extremity, with guidelines as follows:

- If the change in leg length is sudden (i.e., status post orthopedic surgery) and the sacral base was level prior to change, the heel lift should be for the exact amount of sacral base unleveling.
- If the change in leg length is chronic and patient has a flexible spine or mild-to-moderate compensation, the initial heel lift should be 1/8 inch and then adjusted higher by 1/8 inch increments every 2 weeks until the exact amount of sacral base unleveling is reached.
- If the change in leg length is chronic and the patient is considered fragile or has severe compensation, the initial heel lift should be 1/16 inch and then adjusted higher by 1/16 inch increments every 2 weeks until the exact amount of sacral base unleveling is reached.

Evaluation of the Knee

Varus-valgus stress test is used to assess the integrity of the medial and lateral collateral ligaments of the knee. With the patient lying supine, the knee is fully extended. The physician then applies either a varus (medial) or valgus (lateral) strain and assesses for laxity/stability.

Anterior draw test is used to assess for the integrity of the ACL. With the patient lying supine, the patient's knee is flexed to 90°. While sitting on the patient's foot for stability, the physician grasps the proximal tibia with both hands and provides an anterior strain. A positive test is noted when there is anterior shift of the tibia that is significantly greater than the contralateral uninvolved knee. **Lachman's maneuver** is a variation of this. The knee is flexed to only 10°, the distal femur and proximal tibia are grasped, and an anterior strain is introduced to the tibia. Lachman's maneuver is more sensitive than the anterior draw test.

Posterior draw test is used to assess for the integrity of the PCL. It is performed similar to the anterior draw test, except a posterior strain is applied. The results are interpreted as in the anterior draw test.

McMurray test is used to assess for meniscal tears. The physician flexes the patient's knee and rotates the tibia medially and laterally. When the tibia is rotated medially, a varus strain is applied; with lateral rotation, a valgus strain is applied. A positive test elicits a click.

COMLEX Note

The maximum thickness for an insertable heel lift inside the shoe is 1/4 inch. Any amount higher than this needs to be added to the bottom of the shoe to allow it to fit properly.

Apley's compression test is used to assess for meniscal tears. The patient is prone on the exam table. The knee is flexed to 90°. The knee is then compressed by the physician leaning on the patient's heel. At this point, the tibia is rotated medially and laterally. Pain on either side is positive and suggests a meniscal tear on that side.

Patellar femoral grinding is used to assess for possible chondromalacia of the patella. While lying supine, the patient's patella is moved caudad against the tibia. The patient is then asked to contract his/her quadriceps against the physician's resistance. Pain or crepitation is a positive test, and may indicate chondromalacia.

Ballotment is used to assess for possible effusion of the knee. The patella is moved by the physician medially and laterally with the knee extended. The physician observes for fluid moving from side to side in the compartment.

Table 7-2

Test	Positive Finding
Anterior drawer test	Tear of the ACL
Valgus stress test	Tear of the MCL
Varus stress test	Tear of the LCL
McMurray's sign	Tear or displacement of the medial meniscus
Positive compression tests (Apley's)	Meniscus tears
Positive distraction tests (Apley's)	Ligamentous injury
"Bounce home" test (inability to straighten the knee)	Knee effusion
Patellar apprehension test	Dislocating patella

Assessing for Somatic Dysfunction of the Knee

The main objective of assessing the knee joint for dysfunctions is assessing the relationship of the tibia or fibula in respect to the femur.

Tibia

The tibia can be abducted or adducted on the femur. This involves the sliding of the tibia in relation to the femur. This can be assessed by grasping the distal femur and proximal tibia and applying gentle stress to the tibia, either varus (medially) or valgus (laterally). This is similar to testing for MCL or LCL injury, but much less force is used. The side to which the tibia moves more freely is the side of the dysfunction, with the restricted motion being opposite (i.e., abduction dysfunction of the tibia on the femur).

The tibia can also rotate on the femur. This can be assessed the same way as sliding, but instead of applying medial and lateral stress on the tibia, the physician gently applies internal and external motion to the tibia. The direction that has increased rotation is the direction of the dysfunction, with the restricted motion being opposite (i.e., internal rotation dysfunction of the tibia on the femur).

Finally, the tibia can be either anterior or posterior in respect to the femur. This can be assessed the same way anterior/posterior draw assesses for ACL/PCL damage, but with much less force. The direction of increased motion is the direction of the dysfunction, with the restricted motion being opposite (i.e., anterior slide dysfunction of the tibia on the femur).

Fibula

The motion of the fibula is mostly anterior-posterior, so dysfunctions of the fibula are usually in the same directions. With the patient supine, the knee is flexed and the foot is flat on the exam table. The head of the fibula is grasped and anteroposterior motion is applied. The direction of increased slide is the dysfunction, with the restricted motion being opposite (i.e., posterior fibular head). Note that the distal fibula usually slides opposite the dysfunction of the proximal fibular head.

ANKLE AND FOOT

Anatomy

Bones

- Talus
- Calcaneus
- Navicular
- Cuboid
- 3 Cuneiforms
- 5 Metatarsals
- 14 Phalanges

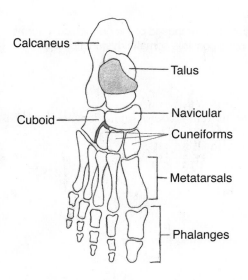

Note the gray area of the talus (the ankle mortise) is wider anteriorly, making the foot more stable in dorsiflexion.

Figure 7-1. Bones of the Foot

Joints

- **Talocrural joint** (tibiotalar joint)—The main motions of this joint are plantar flexion and dorsiflexion. Due to the configuration of the talus (the ankle mortise), the ankle is more stable in dorsiflexion than in plantar flexion. This is the reason that 80% of ankle sprains occur in plantar flexion.
- **Subtalar joint** (talocalcaneal joint)

Arches

Longitudinal arches

- Medial longitudinal arch
- Lateral longitudinal arch

Transverse arch

Somatic dysfunction of the arches usually occur within the transverse arch.

Three somatic dysfunctions of the transverse arch (Figure 7-2):

- **Cuboid**—The medial edge will glide toward the plantar surface.
- **Navicular**—The lateral edge will glide toward the plantar surface.
- **Cuneiforms**—Usually caused by the second cuneiform gliding directly downward, toward the plantar surface.

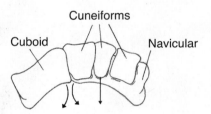

Figure 7-2. Transverse Arch of the Foot. It is composed of the cuboid, cuneiforms, and the navicular. Arrows show 3 possible somatic dysfunctions.

Ligaments

Lateral stabilizers of the ankle (these ligaments prevent excessive supination; *see* Figure 7-3)

- **Anterior talofibular ligament**
- **Calcaneofibular ligament**
- **Posterior talofibular ligament**

Medial stabilizers of the ankle—**Deltoid ligament**

Plantar ligaments—**Spring ligament** (calcaneonavicular ligament)

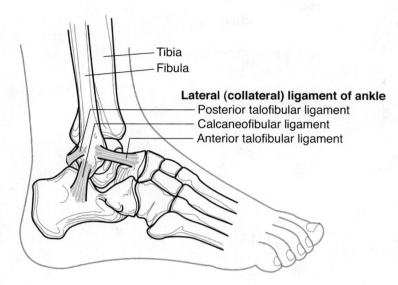

Tibia

Fibula

Lateral (collateral) ligament of ankle
Posterior talofibular ligament
Calcaneofibular ligament
Anterior talofibular ligament

Figure 7-3. Lateral Stabilizers

Craniosacral Motion

8

PRIMARY RESPIRATORY MECHANISM

The cranial field was established by William Garner Sutherland, D.O., D.Sci. (Hon) (1873–1954). As a student, Sutherland noticed that the articular surfaces of the cranial bones had a unique design. After years of research and careful observation, he noticed that the CNS, cerebral spinal fluid (CSF), sacrum, and dural membranes functioned as a unit. He named this unit the primary respiratory mechanism (PRM).

The primary respiratory mechanism involves 5 components:

Inherent motility of the brain and spinal cord. What drives the motion of the brain and spinal cord? Is it due to cellular motion (contraction and relaxation of oligodendrocytes or other cells) within these structures? Or is the motion the result of a yet unmeasured and yet unqualified force interacting with the body?

Fluctuation of the cerebrospinaI fluid. The CSF courses around and throughout the brain and spinal cord, bathing these structures in oxygen and vital nutrients necessary for life. The CSF also moves down the axons, contributing to transneuronal axoplasmic flow. The fluctuation of CSF flow may produce hydraulic pressure waves that are transmitted throughout the body. This may account for the palpable fluctuation that is present both in the head and throughout the body, normally at a rate of 10–14 cycles per minute, but has been reported to be 8–12 cycles per minute. It is important to note that the COMLEX tests the more common rate (10–14 cycles per minute).

Mobility of the intracranial and intraspinal membranes. The dura mater lines the skull and produces folds known as the falx cerebri, falx cerebelli, and tentorium cerebelli. They act as partitions between, and support for, the cerebral hemispheres and cerebellum. They are collectively referred to as the reciprocal tension membrane. This membrane both guides and limits the motion of the various cranial bones. It is through this membrane that a restriction in the motion of one cranial bone can result in altered motion in another cranial bone. The meninges of the spinal cord link the cranium to the sacrum. The entire complex functions as a unit. The dura becomes continuous with the extracranial fascia at various foramina in the base of the skull and continues outward as sheaths (perineurium) surrounding various cranial and spinal nerves.

Articular mobility of the cranial bones. It is commonly believed that the skull is a rigid structure. This point has been debated for years. Many European anatomy texts discuss the articular movement of the cranial sutures. The bevels of the various articular surfaces are intricately designed.

Involuntary mobility of the sacrum between the ilia occurs as the sacrum is suspended between the innominates. The falx cerebri (dura mater) extends inferiorly and firmly attaches to the foramen magnum. It attaches to the bodies of the second and third cervical vertebrae and extends downward as a tube that ultimately attaches to the second sacral segment. Motion of the cranial base is transmitted to and produces palpable motion within the sacrum.

COMLEX Note

CNS + CSF + sacrum + dural membranes = PRM

COMLEX Note

Dural attachments: foramen magnum, C2, C3, and S2

PHYSIOLOGIC MOTION OF THE PRM

Basic Cranial Motion

The adult skull is composed of 29 bones. They can be divided into midline and paired bones. All motions are named relative to the sphenobasilar synchondrosis (SBS). During craniosacral flexion the SBS moves superiorly. The midline bones (sphenoid, occiput, ethmoid, and vomer) move into flexion around their respective transverse axes. The paired bones (temporal, parietal, maxillae, palatine, zygomatic, lacrimal, nasal, inferior conchae) externally rotate about their respective axes. The head expands laterally (gets wider) and the A-P diameter decreases (gets shorter). During craniosacral extension, the reverse occurs.

During **flexion**, the midline bones of the cranium move through a flexion phase. The paired bones of the cranium will move through an external rotation phase.

Flexion at the SBS will cause the dura to be pulled cephalad, moving the sacral base posterior through a transverse axis about S3. This movement at the sacral base (originally termed sacral extension) is called counternutation.

During **extension**, the midline bones of the cranium (sphenoid, occiput, ethmoid, vomer) move through an extension phase. The paired bones of the cranium will move through an internal rotation phase.

Extension at the SBS will cause the dura to be pulled caudad, moving the sacral base anterior through a transverse axis about S3. This movement at the sacral base (originally termed sacral flexion) is called nutation (*see* Figure 8-2).

COMLEX Note

Craniosacral Flexion

1. Flexion of midline bones

2. Sacral counternutation

3. Decreased AP diameter of the cranium

4. Increased lateral diameter of the cranium

5. All paired bones externally rotated

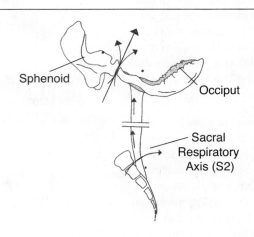

Figure 8-1. Flexion of SBS will cause dura to be pulled cephalad, resulting in counternutation of the sacrum

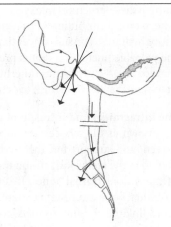

Figure 8-2. Extension of SBS will cause dura to be pulled caudad, resulting in nutation of the sacrum

Table 8-1

	Craniosacral Flexion	**Craniosacral Extension**
Midline bones	Rotates cephalad	Rotates caudad
Paired bones	Externally rotate	Internally rotates
Anteroposterior diameter	Decreases	Increases
Lateral diameter	Increases	Decreases
Sacrum	Counternutates (base rotates posterior)	Nutates (base rotates anterior)

Palpation

The motion of the cranium is commonly evaluated using 2 holds: the vault hold and the fronto-occipital hold.

Vault hold—Patient supine. Sit at the head of the table. You must be comfortable and your hands must be relaxed to palpate these small motions.

1. Index finger on the greater wing of the sphenoid (lateral to the eye).
2. Middle finger on zygomatic process of the temporal bone (in front of ear).
3. Ring finger on mastoid process of temporal bone (in back of ear).
4. Little finger on squamous portion of occipital bone.
5. Thumbs crossed over the sagittal suture (only if comfortable).

Fronto-occipital hold—Patient supine. Sit at the head of the table. One hand supports (is placed beneath) the occiput. The other hand cradles the frontal bone.

Flexion phased—The frontal bone behaves as both a single midline bone (moves into flexion) and as a paired bone by externally rotating (metopic suture gets deeper). The A-P diameter of the head decreases.

Extension phased—The frontal bone moves into extension and internally rotates (metopic suture becomes more shallow). The A-P diameter of the head increases. During flexion the base (top) of the sacrum should press into your fingertips. During extension the apex (bottom) of the sacrum should press into the palm of your hand.

STRAINS OF THE SPHENOBASILAR SYNCHONDROSIS

Torsion

Sphenobasilar torsion is rotation of the base of sphenoid and base of the occiput in opposite directions about an A-P axis. This axis runs from the nasion (midpoint of frontonasal suture) through the center of the SBS to the opisthion (midpoint of posterior border of foramen magnum). Torsions are named for the high greater wing of the sphenoid. The entire orbit may be elevated on the side of the torsion. Torsions can result from trauma to one quadrant of the head, e.g., an upward blow on the cheek, a downward blow on the parietal compressing the parietomastoid suture, or from an occipitomastoid compression.

> **Bridge to Behavioral Science**
>
> A clinically depressed patient usually has a decreased amplitude of the cranial rhythmic impulse (CRI). CV4 treatment is used to increase the amplitude.

COMLEX Note

Know the treatment and uses of

- CV4
- Parietal lift
- Frontal lift
- V spread
- Holds

COMLEX Note

Cranial treatment commonly uses the following approaches:

- Direct
- Indirect
- Balanced membranous tension

Sidebending/Rotation

Involves sidebending through two vertical axes: one through the foramen magnum and one through the body of the sphenoid. The sphenoid and occiput sidebend in opposite directions about these two axes. The two bones sidebend when viewed from above. Named for the direction of motion of the base of the sphenoid. Rotation occurs about an A-P axis running from nasion to opisthion. Both the sphenoid and occiput rotate in the same direction about this A-P axis (the whole mechanism drops inferiorly on one side). Named for the side of the convexity.

To simplify matters, the dysfunction is named for the side of the convexity. During flexion the head will feel fuller on the side of the convexity.

This pattern is named for the direction of freer motion. A sidebending rotation left pattern is present if the right side moves superiorly and produces a concavity (head feels less full on the right side). The left side moves inferiorly and produces a convexity (head feels more full on the left side). Attempting to introduce this motion in the opposite direction is met with restriction.

Lateral Strain

Lateral strain involves rotation about 2 vertical axes: one through the body of the sphenoid and one through the foramen magnum. Refers to a lateral displacement of the base of the sphenoid relative to the base of the occiput. Named for the direction of motion of the base of the sphenoid (direction of freer motion). May result from a traumatic blow to the side of the head anterior or posterior to the plane of the SBS. For example, with a right lateral strain the right hand will easily lift away from the table. Lifting the left hand anteriorly is met with resistance.

Lateral shear is a variant of the lateral strain. It refers to a lateral translation of the base of the sphenoid relative to the base of the occiput. Does not involve rotation about two vertical axes. Test this pattern by holding the occiput with the little fingers. Place your index fingers over the greater wings of the sphenoid. Translate the sphenoid to the left and right with your index fingers. Named for the direction of freer motion. For example, with a right lateral shear the sphenoid will translate freely to the right. Translation to the left is restricted.

Vertical Strain

Vertical strain occurs about two transverse axes (as in flexion/extension): one through the body of the sphenoid and one through the occiput above the level of the jugular process. The base of the sphenoid is carried either superior or inferior relative to the base of the occiput. Named for the direction of motion of the base of the sphenoid. Evaluated using the vault hold. Hold the occiput with your little fingers and translate the sphenoid superior and inferior with your index fingers. There are 2 types:

Superior vertical strain—The sphenoid and occiput rotate in the same direction around parallel transverse axes. The base of the sphenoid is carried superior relative to the base of the occiput. The sphenoid is flexed while the occiput is extended. The sphenoid will translate freely inferiorly. Superior translation is restricted. May result from a traumatic blow on the vertex of the head (posterior to the plane of the SBS) or from below through the mouth (anterior to the plane of the SBS).

Inferior vertical strain—The base of the sphenoid is carried inferior relative to the base of the occiput. The sphenoid is extended while the occiput is flexed. The sphenoid will translate freely superiorly. Inferior translation is restricted. May result from a traumatic blow on the vertex of the head (anterior to the plane of the SBS) or from below through the mouth (posterior to the plane of the SBS).

Compression

SBS compression. The base of the sphenoid is compressed into the base of the occiput. The entire mechanism appears locked. Flexion and extension motions are minimal. The amplitude of the CRI is markedly decreased. The head feels hard. Evaluated using the vault hold. Compression strain of the SBS will result in reduced CRI. It is usually due to trauma, especially to the back of the head.

CRANIAL NERVES

Table 8-2

Nerve	Somatic Dysfunction	Symptoms Associated with Somatic Dysfunction
CN III	Sphenobasilar, facial	Diplopia, ptosis
CN IV	Sphenobasilar, facial	Diplopia when looking down
CN VI	Sphenobasilar, facial	Diplopia
CN VII	Sphenobasilar, facial	Symptoms similar to Bell's palsy
CN VIII	Sphenobasilar, temporal	Tinnitus, vertigo, or hearing loss
CN X	Temporal, occiput, OA, C1, C2, sidebend	Headaches, arrhythmias, GI upset, respiratory problems
CN XII	Sphenobasilar, compression of condylar parts in infants	Dysphagia

Dysfunction of CN IX, X, and XII can cause sucking problems in newborns. Vagal somatic dysfunction can be due to OA, AA, and/or C2 dysfunction.

CRANIOSACRAL TREATMENT

- **Venous sinus technique**
- **CV4: Bulb decompression:** To enhance the amplitude of the CRI.
- **Vault hold**
- **V spread**
- **Lift technique**

Indications for Craniosacral Treatment

Complications

- Headaches
- Tinnitus
- Dizziness
- An alteration in heart rate
- An alteration in blood pressure
- An alteration in respiration
- Gastrointestinal irritability

Contraindications

Absolute contraindications:

- Acute intracranial bleed or increased intracranial pressure
- Skull fracture

Relative contraindications:

- In patients with known seizure history or dystonia, great care must be used in order not to exacerbate any neurologic symptoms.
- Traumatic brain injury

FACILITATION

Facilitation is the maintenance of a pool of neurons (e.g., premotor neurons, motoneurons of preganglionic sympathetic neurons in ≥1 segments of the spinal cord) in a state of partial or subthreshold excitation. In this state, less afferent stimulation is required to trigger the discharge of impulses.

How Does a Segment Become (and Stay) Facilitated?

A spinal cord segment can receive input from 3 areas:

- Higher centers (brain)
- Viscera via sympathetic or parasympathetic visceral afferents
- Somatic afferents (muscle spindles, golgi tendons, nociceptors, etc.)

Any abnormal and steady sensory stimulus from one of these 3 areas can cause the interneurons at a spinal cord level to become sensitive to the stimulus. These "sensitized" interneurons will have an increased or exaggerated output to the initiating site as well as other areas (neighboring muscles or organs via autonomic efferents). Once the sensitized state is established, the segment is then considered to be facilitated. Any continuous sensitizing input or the presence of normal input through sensitized interneurons will maintain the process, allowing the abnormal situation to continue.

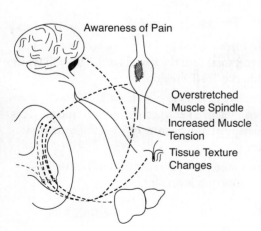

Awareness of Pain

Overstretched Muscle Spindle

Increased Muscle Tension

Tissue Texture Changes

An abnormal sensory stimulus from an overstretched muscle spindle sensitizes two interneurons in the spinal cord. This will result in an increased or exaggerated output to the initiating site (resulting in increased muscle tension), as well as the brain (resulting in an awareness of pain), and local cutaneous tissue (resulting in tissue texture changes).

Figure 9-1. Facilitated Segment

How Does Facilitation Correlate with Somatic Dysfunction?

- Abnormal and continuous sensory input from the overstretched muscle spindle sensitizes the interneurons in the spinal cord at C5.

- A reflex occurs so that muscle tension is produced at the deltoid muscle. This will result in a *restricted* range of motion of the deltoid and *tenderness* upon palpation.

- Prolonged muscle tension causes continuation of the sensitizing input and the maintenance of the facilitated segment.

- Muscle tension at the initiation site (deltoid) causes nociceptor activation in the neighboring areas and a release of bradykinins, serotonin, histamines, potassium, prostaglandins, substance P, and leukotrienes. These substances will cause local vasodilatation and *tissue texture changes*.

- The abnormal and continuous sensory input into C5 may also cause a paraspinal muscle spasm. The resulting increase in muscle tension will cause C5 to rotate or sidebend so that *asymmetry* is present.

Reflexes

Viscerosomatic reflex—According to the *Glossary of Osteopathic Terminology*, a viscerosomatic reflex occurs when localized visceral stimuli produce patterns of reflex response in segmentally related somatic structures.

Somatovisceral reflex—Somatic stimuli may produce patterns of reflex response in segmentally related visceral structures.

Other reflexes

- Somatosomatic
- Viscerovisceral
- Psychosomatic
- Psychovisceral

How Does Facilitation Correlate With These Reflexes?

- Continued gallbladder dysfunction, most often caused by gallstones, will transmit an abnormal sensory input (from visceral receptors) into the spinal cord. This will typically result in segmental facilitation within the T5–T9 region.

- Normal sensory input from general afferents (e.g., muscle spindle) at T5–T9 will become amplified at the sensitized interneurons, resulting in an exaggerated motor response. This will cause an increase in tension in the paraspinal musculature of T5–T9. Tenderness and pain can then be elicited at this region.

- In addition, the increased muscle tension in the paraspinal muscles will cause T5–T9 to rotate and sidebend so that somatic dysfunction is present.

AUTONOMIC INNERVATION

Table 9-1

Structure	Parasympathetic Function	Sympathetic Function
Eye Pupil Lens	Constricts (miosis) Contracts for near vision	Dilates (mydriasis); slight relaxation for far vision
Glands Nasal, lacrimal, parotid, submandibular, gastric, and pancreatic Sweat glands	Stimulates copious secretion (containing many enzymes for enzyme-secreting glands) Sweating on palms of hands	Vasoconstriction for slight secretion Copious sweating (cholinergic)
Heart	Decreases contractility and conduction velocity	Increases contractility and conduction velocity
Lungs Bronchiolar smooth muscle	Contracts	Relaxes

GI tract
 Smooth muscle
  Lumen
  Sphincters
 Secretion and motility
	
	Contracts
	Relaxes
	Increases
		
		Relaxes
		Contracts
		Decreases

Systemic arterioles Skin and visceral vessels Skeletal muscle	None None	Contracts Relaxes
Genitourinary Bladder wall (detrusor) Bladder sphincter (trigone) Penis	Contracts Relaxes Erection	 Contracts Ejaculation
Adrenal medulla		Secretes catacholamines
Liver		Gluconeogenesis Glycogenolysis

COMLEX Note

- Know the **segmental innervation** to each visceral organ.

- Know the **effects of parasympathetic and sympathetic actions**.

Parasympathetic Nervous System

CN III

- Pupils (ciliary ganglion)

CN VII

- Lacrimal and nasal glands (sphenopalatine ganglion [or pterygopalatine])
- Submandibular and sublingual glands (submandibular ganglion)

CN IX

- Parotid gland (otic ganglion)

CN X

- Heart
- Bronchial tree
- Esophagus (lower two-thirds)
- Stomach
- Small intestine
- Liver
- Gallbladder
- Pancreas
- Kidney and upper ureter
- Ovaries and testes
- Ascending and transverse colon

Pelvic splanchnic

- Lower ureter and bladder
- Uterus, prostate, and genitalia
- Descending colon sigmoid and rectum

Table 9-2.

Visceral Organ	Sympathetic Innervation	Parasympathetic Innervation
Head and neck	T1–T4	Cranial nerves III, VII, IX, X
Heart	T1–T5	Vagus n.
Respiratory system	T2–T7	Vagus n.
Esophagus	T2–T8	Vagus n.
Upper GI tract Stomach Liver Gallbladder Spleen Portions of the pancreas and duodenum	T5–T9	Vagus n.
Middle GI tract Portions of the pancreas and duodenum Jejunum Ileum Ascending colon Proximal 2/3 of transverse colon	T9–T12	Vagus n.
Lower GI tract Distal 1/3 of transverse colon Descending colon Sigmoid colon Rectum	T12–L2	S2–S4
Kidneys	T11–L1	Vagus n.
Upper ureters	T10–L1	Vagus n.
Lower ureters	L1–L2	S2–S4
Urinary bladder and urethra	T11–L2	S2–S4
Gonads	T10–T11	Vagus n.
Uterus and cervix	T10–L2	S2–S4
Erectile tissue of penis or clitoris	T11–L2	S2–S4
Extremities Arms	T5–T7	None
Legs	T10–T12	None

Here's an easy way to understand the parasympathetic innervation to organ systems:

Most COMLEX questions will center around which structures are innervated from the vagus nerve vs. the pelvic splanchnic nerve. The following helps you differentiate between the two:

Everything above the diaphragm is innervated by the vagus nerve. Below the diaphragm there are three main organ systems:

- The GI system

- The genitourinary (GU) system

- The reproductive system

In order to remember the innervation to the **GI system**, focus on the large intestine. There are four sections of the large intestine. The ascending, transverse, descending, and recto-sigmoid. Divide the structure in half horizontally. The ascending and transverse colon and all GI-related structures proximal are innervated by the vagus nerve. The descending and recto-sigmoid colon are innervated by the pelvic splanchnic.

To remember the **GU system**, focus on the major visceral structures that the GU system is composed of: the kidneys, the ureters, and the bladder (leave the urethra out of this—it is not a major visceral structure). Divide the system in half horizontally. The kidneys and the upper part of the ureter are innervated by the vagus nerve. The lower part of the ureters and the bladder are innervated by the pelvic splanchnic nerve.

In the **reproductive system**, everything is innervated by the pelvic splanchnic nerve except the gonads (testes or ovaries).

Chapman's Reflexes and Travell's Myofascial Trigger Points

CHAPMAN'S REFLEXES

Chapman's reflexes are a system of reflex points originated by Frank Chapman, D.O. These reflexes are predictable tissue texture abnormalities assumed to be a reflection of visceral dysfunction or pathology.

Chapman's reflex points are **smooth, firm, discretely palpable nodules, approximately 2 to 3 mm in diameter, located within the deep fascia or on the periostium of a bone**.

Chapman's reflexes, in current clinical practice, are used more for diagnosis than for treatment. **They are thought to represent viscerosomatic reflexes**.

COMLEX Note

The appendix Chapman's point is located at the tip of the 12th rib.

Table 10-1

Reflex Point	Location
Appendix	At the tip of the right 12th rib
Adrenals	2 inches superior and 1 inch lateral to the umbilicus and/or the spinous process of T11
Kidneys	1 inch superior and 1 inch lateral to the umbilicus and/or the spinous process of L1
Bladder	At the umbilicus
Colon	Along the femur

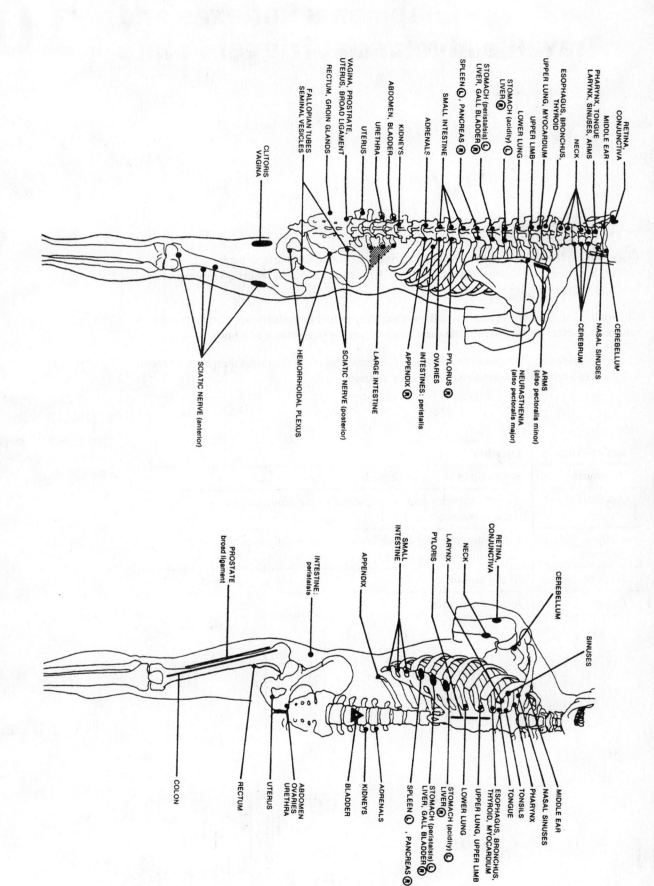

Figure 10-1. Chapman's Reflex Points. (Reproduced with permission from Greyden Press; *Osteopathic Considerations of Systemic Dysfunction* by Michael Kuchera, copyright 1994.)

TRAVELL'S MYOFASCIAL TRIGGER POINTS

A trigger point is a hypersensitive focus, usually within a taut band of skeletal muscle or in the muscle fascia. It is painful upon compression and can give rise to a characteristic referred pain, tenderness, and autonomic phenomena.

Diagnostic Characteristics

Upon compression of the band, the patient will experience pain at the site *and pain referring to an area of the body*.

Pathophysiology

Direct stimuli, such as a muscular strain, overwork fatigue, or postural imbalance can initiate trigger points. Trigger points are a manifestation of a viscero-somatic, somato-visceral, or somato-somato reflex.

Treatment

- Spray and stretch using vapocoolant spray
- Injection with local anesthetic or dry needling
- Muscle energy techniques
- Myofascial release
- Ultrasound
- High voltage galvanic stimulation
- Strain-counterstrain
- Ischemic compression

Trigger Point Versus Tender Point

Tender points are similar to trigger points in that they are taut myofascial bands that are painful upon compression. However, tender points do not refer pain beyond the location compressed.

COMLEX Note

- Trigger points refer pain when pressed.

- Tender points do not refer pain when pressed.

Myofascial Release 11

MYOFASCIAL RELEASE

Myofascial release (MFR) is a form of manual medicine that combines several types of OMT in order to stretch and release muscle (myo) and fascia (fascial) restrictions. Counterstrain, facilitated positional release, unwinding, balanced ligamentous release, functional indirect release, direct fascial release, cranial osteopathy, and visceral manipulation are all forms of myofascial release.

Myofascial release treatment can be direct or indirect, active or passive. It also can be performed anywhere from head to toe because fascia surrounds and compartmentalizes all structures throughout the body.

The goals of myofascial release are to (a) **restore functional balance to all integrative tissues** in the musculoskeletal system, and (b) **improve lymphatic flow by removing myofascial restrictions**.

Typical Myofascial Release Treatment

1. The physician must first palpate a restriction.
2. Once a restriction is palpated, the physician must then decide the type of treatment.
   - In a direct treatment, the physician will move myofascial tissues toward a restrictive barrier.
   - In an indirect treatment, the physician will move myofascial structures away from the restrictive barrier.
3. Then, the physician will add other forces to "fine tune" the treatment:
   - *Twisting* the myofascial structures or applying *transverse forces* perpendicular to the long axis of the muscle.
4. After the physician has correctly addressed the myofascial structures, the patient is asked to use "enhancers" to help induce a release.
5. The physician then awaits a release.

Indications and Contraindications

Myofascial release techniques are typically gentle and can be performed on acutely ill hospitalized patients and elderly patients who cannot tolerate more aggressive therapy. Because these techniques can be done in multiple positions, they also can be done on those who cannot tolerate much movement.

COMLEX Note

Lymphatic techniques, as well as some myofascial release techniques, are contraindicated in patients with cancer because of an increased risk of lymphogenous spread.

There are a few relative contraindications of MFR:

- Bacterial infection (especially if temperature >102°)
- Osseous fracture
- Advanced stages of cancer (risk of spread of metastatic disease)
- Traumatic disruption of visceral organs

Physiologic Diaphragms

There are 4 major diaphragms in the human body. All play a role in lymphatic return (the most important being the abdominal diaphragm).

- Tentorium cerebelli
- Thoracic inlet
- Abdominal diaphragm
- Pelvic diaphragm

MFR Techniques for Improving Lymphatic Flow

MFR can be done to any part of the somatic system. However, not all techniques are directed at improving lymph flow. Restrictions within the diaphragm can theoretically decrease lymph return in two ways. First, if there is limited excursion of the diaphragm, lymph flow will be limited. Second, since the diaphragm is a transverse muscle, it is perpendicular to the lymph channel. If there is restriction within the diaphragm itself, it will shrink the lymph channel.

It is important to release the diaphragm first, then apply lymphatic techniques. If you don't release the diaphragm first, you may be pushing against a restricted diaphragm.

Table 11-1

Junction	Common Compensatory Pattern (80%) Rotation	Uncommon Compensatory Pattern (20%) Rotation
Occipitoatlantal	Left	Right
Cervicothoracic	Right	Left
Thoracolumbar	Left	Right
Lumbosacral	Right	Left

Lymphatic Treatment

The body has a second circulatory system other than the arterio-venous system that circulates fluid. This second system is the lymphatic system. Lymph is a milky, white fluid composed of fat, fatty acids, glycerol, and proteins that circulates around the body in vessels. These vessels have unidirectional valves to direct proper flow. The lymphatic system also has nodes, which are local collecting centers in most parts of the body.

There are many functions of the lymphatic system, but there are 2 functions that are pivotal to general health, and that can be influenced by osteopathic manipulation.

- Clearance of extracellular fluid and proteins, thus preventing edema and fluid accumulation
- Combating infections, particularly clearing infectious agents, transferring these agents to immune centers, and transporting immune cells (macrophages, T and B cells, etc.) to sites where they are needed

Anatomy and Flow

Generally, lymph flows from superficial parts of the body to deep parts of the body. The local regions that are lymph centers for superficial purposes are the cervical, axillary, and inguinal lymph node chains. Internal organs below the diaphragm eventually drain into the thoracic duct that traverses through Sibson's Fascia at C7 (thoracic inlet) and eventually joins the left main duct. The left lymphatic (or major) duct drains most organs and regions except for the right upper extremity, the right hemicranium, the heart, and the lobes of the lung (except the left upper lobe). These regions and organs drain into the right (or minor) lymphatic duct. The left duct usually drains into the subclavian vein at its junction the left internal jugular. The right duct drains similarly on the right side; however, there are normal anatomic variations on the right side.

Muscle contraction and compartment pressures are the main factors that help lymphatic flow. Thus, exercise, breathing, and diaphragmatic contraction all affect lymphatic flow. Soft tissue restrictions or contractions where the lymph vessels pass through can impede flow. Sympathetic input also causes constriction of the lymphatic vessels, thus decreasing flow. These are points where osteopathic manipulation is pivotal.

Treatments

Thoracic pump (a.k.a. Pump of Miller) is used to enhance flow in the thoracic cavity. The physician directly enhances exhalation, and in doing so indirectly increases the negative thoracic pressure on inhalation. This increases lymphatic and venous flow to the right side of the heart.

Pedal pump enhances flow by cyclic pulsations of the patient's feet leading to fluid waves throughout the body.

Thoracic inlet release releases the soft tissue of the thoracic inlet and enhances lymphatic flow by decreasing the constriction around the thoracic duct. Commonly, C7 is treated, as well as the scalenes and the clavicle. Sibson's fascia is directly attached to the posterior aspect of the clavicle, so a common treatment is superior traction of the clavicle to stretch and release the fascia behind it.

Rib raising increases the motion of the rib cage, and normalizes sympathetic input (sympathetic chain ganglia lie behind the heads of the ribs). Rib raising is very effective for pneumonia, post-op ileus, and bronchitis due to modulation of sympathetic output.

Extremity fluid wave improves fluid motion in an extremity. The treatment consists of wave like motions of the involved extremity toward the closest lymphatic center. This is very commonly used in breast cancer patients after mastectomy with axillary dissection. After the surgery, many of these patients develop edema of the involved upper extremity; this treatment helps relieve the edema.

Redoming the diaphragm improves diaphragmatic function and thus lymphatic flow.

Spleen and liver pump: liver and spleen are organs that respond to physical pressure by increasing their activities; with these treatments, the physician directly pumps the spleen and liver, increasing circulation, lymphatic and antibody production, and antigen clearance.

Lymphatic treatments can be used in most infectious and fluid overload disorders. Liver and spleen pump are contraindicated in patients with infectious mononucleosis due to risk of splenic rupture. The treatments are also contraindicated in patients with suspected abscesses, and any type of cancer due to the risk of spread.

COUNTERSTRAIN

Counterstrain is a **passive indirect technique** in which the tissue being treated is positioned at a point of balance or ease away from the restrictive barrier.

A **tender point** is a small tense edematous area of tenderness about the size of a fingertip. It is typically located near bony attachments of tendons and ligaments or in the belly of some muscles.

Basic Counterstrain Treatment Steps

1. Locate a significant tender point.
2. Palpate the tender points.
3. Place the patient in the position of optimal comfort, shortening the muscle.

    Maverick point: Approximately 5% of tender points will not improve with the expected treatment, even with careful fine tuning. These Maverick points are treated by positioning the patient in a position opposite of what would be typically used.

4. With the patient completely relaxed, maintain the position of comfort for 90 seconds.
5. Slowly return to neutral.
6. Recheck the tender point.

COUNTERSTRAIN TECHNIQUES

Cervical Spine

Anterior cervical tender points

Location: the lateral aspect or slightly anterior to the lateral mass (articular pillar) of the vertebrae

Posterior cervical tender points

Location: usually at the tip of the spinous process or on the lateral sides of the spinous process

Cervical Counterstrain Treatments

Almost all counterstrain treatments for the cervical spine, whether anterior or posterior, follow one of two motions:

Sidebend Away and Rotate Away (SARA)

> or

Sidebend Toward and Rotate Away (STAR)

SARA is the most common, so any points requiring STAR are considered maverick points. Despite these positions, the most important aspect of counterstrain treatment is to move the tender point into a position of the least tenderness, regardless of the adjustments required to do so.

Table 12-1

Anterior	
Tender Point	**Position**
AC1	Marked rotation away
AC2	Slight flexion + SARA
AC3	Slight flexion + SARA
AC4	Flexion + SARA
AC5	Flexion + SARA
AC6	Flexion + SARA
AC7 (Maverick point)	Flexion + STAR
AC8	Flexion + SARA
Posterior	
Tender Point	**Position**
PC1 (inion)	Marked flexion
PC1 occiput	Extension
PC2	Extension
PC3 (maverick point)	Flexion + SARA
PC4	Extension + SARA
PC5	Extension + SARA
PC6	Extension + SARA
PC7	Extension + SARA
PC8	Extension + SARA

Thoracic Spine

Anterior thoracic tender points

Locations:

- T1–T6: located at the midline of the sternum at the attachment of the corresponding ribs
- T7–T12: most are located in the rectus abdominus muscle about one inch lateral to the midline on the right or left.

Posterior thoracic tender points

Location: on either side of the spinous process or on the transverse process

Thoracic Counterstrain Treatments

Anterior

Anterior tenderpoints from T1-6 are treated primarily with flexion, with minor rotation or side-bending. Anterior tenderpoints from T7-12 are treated with flexion, sidebending towards, and rotation either of the torso away from the tenderpoint, or the pelvis towards the tenderpoint.

Posterior

All posterior thoracic spinous process tender points are treated with extension while the patient is prone. All posterior thoracic transverse process tender points are treated with extension + SART.

Ribs

Anterior tender points are associated with anteriorly depressed ribs (also called exhalation ribs, an exhalation dysfunction, or an inhalation restriction). Posterior tender points are associated with posteriorly depressed ribs (also called inhalation ribs, an inhalation dysfunction, or an exhalation restriction).

Anterior rib tender points

Locations:

- Rib 1: tender point is located just below the medial end of the clavicle
- Rib 2: tender point is 6 to 8 cm lateral to the sternum on rib 2
- Ribs 3–6: located along the mid-axillary line on the corresponding rib

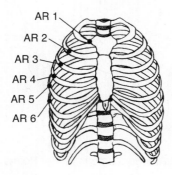

Figure 12-1. Anterior Rib Tender Points

Posterior rib tender points

Location: the angle of the corresponding rib

Rib Counterstrain Treatments

Table 12-2

Anterior	
Tender Point	**Position**
Rib 1 (depressed, exhalation dysfunction)	Head flexed and rotated and sidebent toward tender point
Rib 2 (depressed, exhalation dysfunction)	Head flexed and rotated and sidebent toward tender point
Rib 3-6	Flex, sidebend and rotate toward tender point
Posterior	
Tender Point	**Position**
Rib 1 (elevated, inhalation dysfunction)	Sidebend away, rotate toward, and slightly extend
Rib 2-6	SARA with slight flexion

Lumbar Spine

Anterior lumbar tender points

Locations:
- L1: medial to the ASIS
- L2–L4: on the AIIS
- L5: 1 cm lateral to the pubic symphysis on the superior ramus

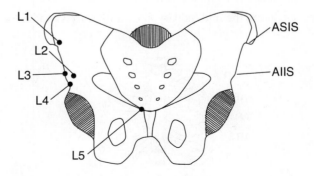

Figure 12-2. Anterior Lumbar Tender Points

Posterior lumbar tender points

Location: on either side of the spinous process or on the transverse process. L3 and L4 may be found on the iliac crest. Also, L5 may be found on the PSIS.

Lumbar Counterstrain Treatments

Anterior

Anterior lumbar tender points are treated with significant flexion and rotation away from the tender point. The flexion is accomplished by having the patient supine, with knees and hips flexed, and the physician manipulating the angles of flexion. L2 also has an abdominal tender point, which is treated with flexion as well, but rotated toward the tender point.

Posterior

The posterior lumbar tender points generally require extension and sidebending away to release. Lower Pole L5 is a maverick point that requires the patient prone with the same side leg off the table, hip and knee flexed, and rotated toward the tender point.

Pelvis

Iliacus

Location: approximately 7 cm medial to the ASIS

Sacrum and Pelvis Counterstrain Treatments

Anterior

- Low ilium sacroiliac/anterior sacral tender point: patient is supine, thigh is flexed
  Iliacus tender point: patient is supine, thigh is flexed and externally rotated; this tenderpoint often associated with dysmenorrhea
- Inguinal ligament: patient is supine, legs are flexed and rested on the physician's thigh; leg closest to physician is crossed over opposite leg, and lower leg is used as a lever by being internally rotated

Posterior

- Piriformis: patient is prone with same side leg off the edge of the table, patient's hip and knee are flexed, and leg is externally rotated and abducted; this tender point is associated with sciatica
- High flare-out sacroiliac tender point: patient is prone, and leg of the same side of tender point is extended, with some adduction/external rotation required at times; this tender point is associated with coccygodynia

MUSCLE ENERGY TREATMENTS

Muscle energy is a form of OMT in which the patient actively uses his muscles, on request, "from a precisely controlled position in a specific direction, against a distinctly executed counterforce."

Types of Muscle Energy

- Bone movement (articular)
- Postisometric relaxation
- Reciprocal inhibition
- Respiratory assistance
- Oculocephalogyric reflex

Postisometric relaxation

The physician moves the joint into the barrier in all planes. We will use the biceps as an example. The physician extends the elbow to the restrictive barrier, then the patient isometrically contracts. The definition of isometric contraction is that the origin and insertion stays the same but the tension is increased. The golgi tendon senses an increase in tension and sends impulses back to the spinal cord, allowing the muscle extrafusal fibers to relax.

Reciprocal inhibition

By contracting the antagonistic muscle, signals are transmitted to the spinal cord and through the reciprocal inhibition reflex arc; the agonist muscle is then forced to relax.

Oculocephalogyric reflex

The patient uses eye motions to activate or deactivate various cervical muscles.

Muscle Energy Treatment Procedure for Postisometric Relaxation Approach

1. The physician positions the bone or joint so the muscle group will engage the restrictive barrier (direct treatment) in all planes of motion.
2. The operator instructs the patient to reverse direction in one or all planes of motion.
3. The patient contracts the appropriate muscle(s) or muscle group with the objective of moving the body part through a complete range of motion.
4. The physician maintains an appropriate counterforce so that the contraction is perceived at the critical articulation or area for 3 to 5 seconds.
5. The physician then instructs the patient to relax and the physician also relaxes. Then, during the postisometric relaxation phase, the physician takes up the slack, allowing it to be passively lengthened. Increased range of motion is noted by the physician.
6. Steps 1 through 5 are repeated three to five times until the best possible increase in motion is obtained.

Contraindications

Postsurgical patients, intensive care patients, and patients who cannot or will not follow directions.

Muscle Energy Techniques

- Cervical spine
- Upper thoracic: use head as lever for T1–T4
- Lower thoracic and lumbar spine: move torso to induce motion of the vertebral column
- Ribs

Exhalation Dysfunctions

There are many different methods used when treating exhalation dysfunctions. Techniques differ slightly. The important concept of these rib treatments is to keep in mind which muscle is being used to correct the dysfunction.

- Rib 1: Patient raises head directly toward ceiling.
- Rib 2: Patient turns head 30° away from dysfunctional side and lifts head toward ceiling.
- Ribs 3–5: Patient pushes elbow of affected side toward the opposite ASIS.
- Ribs 6–9: Push arm anterior.
- Ribs 10–12: Patient adducts arm.

Table 13-1

Ribs	Muscles
Rib 1	Anterior and middle scalenes
Rib 2	Posterior scalene
Ribs 3–5	Pectoralis minor
Ribs 6–9	Serratus anterior
Ribs 10–12	Latissimus dorsi

OA Dysfunctions

When treating OA dysfunctions, the barriers are engaged and the contractions used for treatment are resisted using the patient's chin.

- Chin to chest: Flexion
- Chin to ceiling: Extension

Muscle Energy for the Sacrum and Pelvis

Anterior Iliac-Innominate-Pelvic Dysfunction

This dysfunction can be treated from the prone or supine position. The main point of the treatment is that the patient **extends the knee and hip against physician resistance** for 3-5 seconds. Treatment is repeated 3-5 times, each time further engaging the restrictive barrier. The dysfunction is then reassessed.

Posterior Iliac-Innominate-Pelvic Dysfunction

This dysfunction can be treated from the prone or supine position. The main point of the treatment is that the patient **flexes the hip against physician resistance** for 3-5 seconds. Treatment is repeated 3-5 times, each time further engaging the restrictive barrier. The dysfunction is then reassessed.

Superior Pubic Dysfunction

The patient is supine. The patient has the leg of the same side as the dysfunction off the side of the exam table. The physician abducts the leg off the side of the table until resistance is met. The opposite ASIS is stabilized. The patient then flexes the thigh toward the opposite ASIS against physician resistance for 3-5 seconds. Treatment is repeated 3-5 times, each time further engaging the restrictive barrier. The dysfunction is then reassessed.

Inferior Pubic Dysfunction

The patient is supine. The physician flexes and abducts the patient's hip and knee until motion and resistance is ascertained. The patient is then instructed to extend and adduct (straighten out the leg) against physician resistance for 3-5 seconds. Treatment is repeated 3-5 times, each time further engaging the restrictive barrier. The dysfunction is then reassessed.

Unilateral Sacral Flexion

The patient is prone. The physician places the heel of his or her hand on the patient's ILA of the same side of the dysfunction. The patient is asked to inhale and to hold that breath. At this point, the physician pushes cephalad and toward the table for 3-5 seconds. The patient is then asked to exhale, and the physician resists any movement by the sacrum. Treatment is repeated 3-5 times, each time further engaging the restrictive barrier. The dysfunction is then reassessed.

Unilateral Sacral Extension

The patient is prone. The physician places the heel of his or her hand on the patient's sacral sulcus of the side of the dysfunction. The patient is asked to exhale and to hold that breath. At this point, the physician pushes caudad toward the table for 3-5 seconds. The patient is then asked to inhale, and the physician resists any movement by the sacrum. Treatment is repeated 3-5 times, each time further engaging the restrictive barrier. The dysfunction is then reassessed.

Forward Sacral Torsion

The patient is lying chest down with torso, hips, and knees flexed (lateral Sims position) with the side of the axis in the dysfunction on the table. The physician flexes the patient's hips until motion is elicited at the lumbosacral junction. The patient's legs are dropped off the exam table to induce sidebending. The patient is then asked to raise his/her legs toward the ceiling for 3-5 seconds. With the free hand, the physician monitors the sacrum for posterior movement. Treatment is repeated 3-5 times, each time further engaging the restrictive barrier. The dysfunction is then reassessed.

Backward Sacral Torsion

The patient is lying with the side of the axis of dysfunction on the table, and upper torso facing the ceiling (lateral recumbent position). The physician flexes the patient's hips until motion is elicited in the lumbosacral junction. The patient's legs are dropped off the exam table to induce sidebending. The patient is then asked to raise the legs toward the ceiling for 3-5 seconds. With the free hand, the physician monitors the sacrum for anterior movement. Treatment is repeated 3-5 times, each time further engaging the restrictive barrier. The dysfunction is then reassessed.

Muscle Energy for the Upper Extremities

Posterior Radial Head

Radial head is free in pronation, and restricted in supination. With the patient seated, the physician holds the distal end of the patient's forearm. The physician passively supinates until resistance is met. The patient is then asked to pronate against physician resistance for 3-5 seconds. The barrier is then re-engaged and the pronation is repeated 3-5 times. The radial head is then reassessed.

Anterior Radial Head

Radial head is free in supination, and restricted in pronation. With the patient seated, the physician holds the distal end of the patient's forearm. The physician passively pronates until resistance is met. The patient is then asked to supinate against physician resistance for 3-5 seconds. The barrier is then re-engaged and the supination is repeated 3-5 times. The radial head is then reassessed.

High Velocity/Low Amplitude $\quad$ 14

GENERAL PROCEDURE

High velocity/low amplitude (HVLA) is a **passive, direct technique** that uses high velocity/low amplitude forces to remove motion loss in a somatic dysfunction. After positioning a restricted joint against its restrictive barrier, a short (low amplitude) quick (high velocity) thrust is directed to move the joint past the restrictive barrier. HVLA techniques may also be called thrust techniques or mobilization with impulse treatment.

1. After correct diagnosis of a somatic dysfunction, the physician will move the dysfunctional segment in such a way that it is against its restrictive barrier. This is ideally done by reversing all three planes of motion. *Note*: Due to the facet orientation and biomechanics in certain regions of the spine, it is not always possible to reverse all three planes of motion (i.e., the cervical spine). See specific HVLA techniques for details.

2. The patient is then asked to relax. If the patient is not relaxed, the treatment will fail and the corrective thrust may cause soft tissue damage. The exhalation phase of respiration is the relaxation phase, and the final force is often applied during exhalation.

3. The physician then uses a short, quick thrust to move the dysfunctional segment through the restrictive barrier. Often a pop or click is heard along with an increase in the range of motion. *Be sure to remain against the restrictive barrier before applying the thrust. Do not back off before the thrust.*

4. Re-evaluate range of motion.

INDICATIONS AND CONTRAINDICATIONS

Indications

Treatment of motion loss in somatic dysfunction. Not ordinarily indicated for treatment of joint restriction due to pathologic changes such as contractures or advanced degenerative joint disease.

Absolute Contraindications

- Osteoporosis
- Osteomyelitis (including Pott's disease)
- Fractures in the area of thrust (remember spondylolysis and spondylolisthesis)
- Bone metastases (HVLA may result in a pathologic fracture)
- Severe rheumatoid arthritis

COMLEX Note

Safety is related to the distance that the joint moves during the thrust. The shorter the distance, the safer the technique.

COMLEX Note

Know the absolute and relative contraindications for HVLA.

Relative Contraindications

- Acute whiplash
- Pregnancy
- Postsurgical conditions
- Herniated nucleus propulsis
- Patients on anticoagulation therapy or hemophiliacs should be treated with great caution to prevent bleeding.
- Vertebral artery ischemia (cervical HVLA only)

COMPLICATIONS

Minor Complications

Most common: soreness or symptom exacerbation

Major Complications

Most common overall: vertebral artery injury. These problems usually arise with the use of cervical rotatory forces with the neck in the extended position.

Most common in the low back: cauda equina syndrome (very rare)

SPECIFIC HVLA TREATMENTS

Cervical

OA

For example, C4 FR_LS_R. In order to treat this somatic dysfunction, the cervical spine must be extended down to C4; C4 must then be rotated right, and sidebent left. A corrective (often sidebending) thrust is applied to the segment.

AA

For example, AAR_R. To correct this somatic dysfunction, the head is flexed 45° then rotated to the left. A rotatory corrective thrust is then applied to the left.

Typical cervical segments (C2–C7)

These cervical segments can be treated by using either a sidebending or rotatory thrust. Because these upper segments prefer rotation, typically a rotatory HVLA thrust is used to correct dysfunction. The lower cervical segments prefer sidebending; therefore, a sidebending HVLA thrust works well.

As a general rule, to limit motion of (lock out) the facets above the dysfunction, the physician must rotate toward the barrier when using a sidebending thrust or sidebend toward the barrier when using a rotational thrust.

Thoracics and Ribs

The thoracic segments and ribs can be treated with HVLA in many positions. The position most commonly taught at osteopathic medical schools has been nicknamed the Kirksville Krunch. This technique is easy to understand and versatile. With very little modification of technique, the Kirksville Krunch can treat most thoracic and rib dysfunctions.

When treating a flexed lesion, the corrective force will be directed at the dysfunctional segment, and the thrust is aimed toward the floor. When treating an extended lesion, the corrective thrust is directed at the vertebrae below the dysfunctional segment, and the thrust is aimed 45° cephalad. A neutral lesion is treated the same way as a flexed dysfunction; however, sidebend the patient away from you. A purely flexed or extended lesion (no rotation or sidebending) is treated using roughly the same position, except the physician will use a bilateral fulcrum (thenar eminence under one transverse process and a flexed MCP under the other transverse process). Ribs 2–10 can also be treated using the Kirksville Krunch. The difference is that the physician's thenar eminence is under the posterior rib angle of the "key" rib.

Lumbar Spine

T10–L5 may be treated with HVLA using the "lumbar roll." Flexion, extension, or neutral lesions can all be treated in the same lateral recumbent position. The physician may treat the patient with the posterior transverse up or the posterior transverse process down. For example, if L3 were FRS_R, the physician could treat the patient in the left lateral recumbent position (posterior transverse process up) or in the right lateral recumbent position (transverse process down). There is only one modification with the patient's position between the two treatments, summarized in Table 14-1.

Table 14-1

Lumbar Roll Treatment
Type II Dysfunction
If treating the patient with the transverse process up → pull the patient's inferior arm down
If treating the patient with the transverse process down → pull the patient's inferior arm down
Type I Dysfunction
If treating the patient with the transverse process up → pull the patient's inferior arm up
If treating the patient with the transverse process down → pull the patient's inferior arm down

ARTICULATORY TECHNIQUES

Articulatory techniques (also called springing techniques or low velocity/moderate amplitude techniques) are direct techniques that increase range of motion in a restricted joint. The physician engages the restrictive barrier and uses gentle repetitive forces to increase range of motion within that joint.

Postoperative patients and elderly patients find articulatory techniques more acceptable than other vigorous types of direct techniques because articulating forces are gentle in nature.

Indications

- Limited or lost articular motion. Elderly patients with shoulder problems (adhesive capsulitis) will benefit from the seven stages of Spencer. Muscle energy can also be incorporated into this treatment to loosen shoulder muscles.
- Need to increase frequency or amplitude of motion of a body region (for example, the need to increase frequency and amplitude of chest wall motion in a person with respiratory disease).
- The need to normalize sympathetic activity (rib raising technique). Rib raising will stimulate sympathetics as well as increase chest wall motion.

Contraindications

- Repeated hyper-rotation of the upper cervical spine when positioned in extension may cause damage to the vertebral artery.
- Acutely inflamed joint, especially where the cause of the inflammation may be from an infection or fracture.

Typical Articulatory Procedures

1. Move the affected joint to the limit of all ranges of motion. Once a restrictive barrier is reached, slowly and firmly continue to apply gentle force against it.
2. At this time, you may use respiratory cooperation or muscle energy activation to further increase myofascial stretch of tight tissues.
3. Return the articulation to its neutral position.
4. Repeat the process several times.
5. Cease repetition of motion when no further response is achieved.

Spencer Techniques

The Spencer technique (or 7 Stages of Spencer) is useful in patients who have developed fibrosis and restriction during a period of inactivity (adhesive capsulitis) following an injury. Such injuries may include a healed rotator cuff tear or immobilization of the shoulder girdle after a humerus fracture.

The Spencer techniques are performed in 7 stages:

Stage I: extension of the upper extremity with the elbow flexed

Stage II: flexion of the upper extremity with the elbow extended

Stage III: circumduction with slight compression and the elbow flexed

Stage IV: circumduction with traction with the elbow extended

Stage V: abduction with internal rotation; adduction with external rotation

Stage VI: abduction and internal rotation with the upper extremity behind the back

Stage VII: stretching tissues and pumping fluids with the arm extended